Mapping Memories

Reminiscence with Ethnic Minority Elders

An Age Exchange Publication
Edited by Pam Schweitzer

Published by Age Exchange March 2004

11 Blackheath Village, London SE3 9LA
Tel 020 8318 9105, Fax 020 8318 0060
administrator@age-exchange.org.uk
www.age-exchange.org.uk

ISBN 0 947860 29 0
British Library Cataloguing
in Publication Data
A catalogue record for this book is
available from the British Library

PRODUCTION

Editor Pam Schweitzer
Research Meena Khatwa
Creative Activities Sections
Pam Schweitzer
Cover & Text Design, Editorial Assistance
Lionel@Openshaw.uk.net
Interviews Meena Khatwa with
Ernest Bangura, Indie Choudhury
Venla Hellstedt, Pam Schweitzer
Jean Valsler and David Saville
Transcription Meena Khatwa
Ernest Bangura, Indie Choudhury
David Schweitzer, Emma Newton
Jean Valsler, Venla Hellstedt
Story Editors
Meena Khatwa, Pam Schweitzer
Photography Rado Klose
Alex Schweitzer, Meena Khatwa
Donna Henry, Helen Kon
Printing Tower Printing Company Ltd

FUNDING

Age Exchange gratefully acknowledges financial support from the following
The Community Fund
The Bridge House Trust
South Greenwich Regeneration Agency
London Development Agency
London Borough of Greenwich
London Borough of Lewisham

LIFE STORY TELLERS

Chinese Elders
Mr Ke Wing Pang, Mrs Phuong La
Mrs Ah Poh Luong, Mrs Mooi Tran
Mrs Makfung San, Mrs Suk Tsang Tang

African Elders
Mrs Belmont Williams
Mrs Josephine Macpeppele Ja Ja
Mr Ade Aderogba
Mr Anthony Maduagwu
Mr James Adebayo Adesina
Mrs Mako Herabe, Mrs Hawa Ismail Mumin

Caribbean Elders
Mrs Irma Reid, Mr Michael Roper
Mrs Gladys Smith, Mrs Hyacinth Thomas
Mrs May Gladys Berry

Asian Elders
Mr Santi Rakhit, Mrs Sheila Rakhit
Mrs Avtar Bilkhu, Mr Fazal Rahim Shah
Mr Bagwant Singh, Mrs Pramila Desai

Film Interviewees
Vina & Nirpal Loyal, Mrs Annette Akporiaye
Mrs Siu Lan Voong, Mrs Choy Wah Liu
Mrs Quan Vong, Mrs Tai Chai Luong
Carl & Joan Scantlebury

AGE EXCHANGE BLACK & ETHNIC MINORITIES ELDERS PROJECT

Project Coordinator Meena Khatwa
Project Administrator Indie Choudhury
Project Manager Pam Schweitzer
Project Supervisors
Satya Devi Paul, Ade Aderogba
Creative Activities Coordination
Meena Khatwa, Pam Schweitzer
Festival Organisation
Meg Hamilton, Victoria John
Pam Schweitzer, Frances Scott
Arthur Torrington, Geoff Garvey

Creative Arts Workers
Madhumita Bose, Ajay Chhabra
Simmy Gupta, Kinga Hajnal
Donna Henry, Erene Kaptani
Sharon Morgan, Mia Morris
Donna Pieters, Lotta Petronella
Peggy Pettitt, Joscelin Platt
Alex Schweitzer,Pam Schweitzer
Thelma Sharma, Jean Valsler
Kaiya Williams, Steve Wilson

Film Makers
Jean Valsler
Lotta Petronella

Group Leaders
Helen Kon
Kenneth Lee Sheltered Housing Scheme
Amelia Soodoo and Nassim Khodabux
Elford Close African & Caribbean Day Centre
Satya Devi Paul, *Saheli Women's Group and Ramgharia Sikh Temple, Woolwich*
Sahra Ali, *Somali Resource & Cultural Centre*
Atia Malik, *Asra Sheltered Housing*
Joan Scantlebury
Caribbean Over-Fifties Association
Surjit Juthla, *Sehmi Day Centre*
Terry Chan, *Deptford Indo-Chinese Group*
Anthony Maduagwu
Ajoda African Elders' Group
Zeinab Mahmood
Ferrier Somali Women's Group
Annette Akporiaye
Dorcas African Elders' Group

Many thanks to Professor Faith Gibson, for editorial help.

This book is dedicated with grateful thanks to the elders who gave us their time and stories.

Films on the enclosed disk:

Long Ago and Far Away
Examples of creative activities sessions in progress

Life Portraits
The lives past and present of seven elders

Contents

Foreword

By Alex Kalache MD, PhD
Coordinator – Ageing & Life Course
World Health Organisation, Geneva

Reminiscence is a health-giving activity – as Age Exchange has demonstrated through its many inspiring projects over the last twenty years both in the United Kingdom and across Europe. As I grow older away from my home country, I increasingly appreciate the importance of reminiscing: it is a process that gives us a sense of our individuality, a feeling of shared experience and mutual support to our group, and it provides a sense of history to the wider community.

Demographically speaking, older people are an ever more significant element in the British society. Yet their voices are not heard loud enough and their experiences not adequately valued – least of all foreign elderly people. We have witnessed tremendous population movements in the second half of the twentieth century. As a result, the numbers of people growing old far from their native homes have increased sharply. Yet, the provision of appropriate resources and services to meet their needs is only slowly catching up with this emerging reality. With its new book, *Mapping Memories*, Age Exchange opens a window on to the lives of ethnic minority elders in Britain. Its imaginative suggestions for creative activities around life experience represent an important resource for the future.

The stories were collected from a small area of south east London, but they take us across the world from the Caribbean to Africa, India and China, reminding us what a rich and under-used asset Britain has through this cultural patchwork. The lessons from these life stories go beyond the British borders. Migration was a vibrant reality of the second half of last century and will continue to be a driving force in the construction of tomorrow's societies across the developed world. And we should all be glad for that – it results in much richer, more diverse and dynamic communities. It is important that younger generations in our ethnically mixed societies develop an understanding of the forces which have created and continue to create such a mix.

The memories of the 'ordinary' people in this book, include struggles to escape danger, war, hunger and poverty, the sometimes painful and sometimes comical business of learning the ways of a new country, often in a new language. They tell us of the need to cope with feelings of loss and displacement, the great acts of will required to build new lives far from home, and the hope of a better future for their children.

Once again, Age Exchange is leading the way by recording the past of a whole generation of ethnic minority elders, preserving it for our own future.

Saheli Women's Group partaking in a dance-based reminiscence exercise

Introduction

By Pam Schweitzer

This book is about memories and reminiscence activities. It contains fascinating life stories told by older people from ethnic minority groups, and provides some starting points for reminiscence work. It has been produced to support the work of the many organisations, both statutory and voluntary, which provide meeting places, meals and activities for ethnic elders, in order to combat the loneliness and lack of stimulation which can accompany old age. These community, education, health and faith organisations give a new focus to older people who have lost the structure of their working lives and the companionship it provided. In many cases, they have also lost key family members through bereavement or relocation.

Reminiscence

Reminiscence sessions, and the creative activities arising from them, can make an enjoyable and enriching contribution to the programmes on offer to ethnic

Preparing a show – BASCA Elders' Group remembering old songs from the Caribbean

minority elders. It is natural in later life to think back and reconnect with the people, places and events of one's past. This process helps to make sense of one's life as a whole, reviewing it constructively, valuing one's experience and coming to terms with the present. For elders who are physically removed from the countries where they grew up, it is particularly valuable to reminisce with others from a similar culture and background about their younger days, which are often remembered so sharply and poignantly in old age.

There is little suitable resource material currently available relating to reminiscence with ethnic minority elders. We hope therefore that the stories we have gathered and the activities we have suggested will help to fill this gap, acting as a stimulus for further reminiscence, discussion and creative work. The book is also intended to offer younger readers a chance to listen to and learn from the life journeys of these older people, and to increase their own understanding of different cultures. With these objectives in mind, many ideas have been included to encourage reminiscence-related classroom activities, particularly inter-generational learning journeys.

Life Stories

We have interviewed older people from India and Pakistan, the Caribbean, Africa and the Far East, who settled in Britain in the second half of the twentieth century. The interviews were conducted in people's own homes or in community and day centres. We are extremely grateful to the group leaders, translators and others who helped facilitate this work.

The life-stories come from twenty-four elders, although ten times that number have participated in the group reminiscence sessions and creative arts activities we have run as part of the project. The culmination of this creative work was a three-day inter-cultural festival of reminiscence arts in which the groups of ethnic minority elders presented plays, films and exhibitions based on their past lives and worked together in practical arts workshops.

We asked all the interviewees to tell us about significant stages in their lives:

- their home and family in the country of their birth;
- the circumstances of their growing up and their education;
- their courting days and marriage;
- their decision to leave home and their journey to Britain;
- their early years in their new country;
- their experience of growing old in Britain.

The book has been arranged in chapters around these key stages. Many of the story-tellers appear in every chapter, so that the reader can follow their stories through from childhood to old age. Within each chapter, it is interesting to

Cultural exchange – black and white pensioners rehearsing together

compare and contrast experience from across countries and cultures. People from the same or related cultures have been grouped together, so that anyone working with elders from the same corner of the world will have several examples to draw on to stimulate their group. Sometimes the experiences differ widely within a culture and across cultures, and we hope that this will help to prevent stereotyping and break down preconceptions and prejudices.

Creative Follow-Up

Each chapter is followed by suggestions for activities designed to deepen the level of discussion and increase mutual understanding between the elders. Suggestions are also included in each chapter for educational and for inter-generational activities related to key areas of the National Curriculum such as history, geography, social studies, English and citizenship. There is also much potential for using the material in the weekend schools that many ethnic minority communities have established to teach young people the language, customs, faiths, music and dances of their families' country of origin. Emphasis has been placed on creative exploration of the stories through drama, art and creative writing, but there are also many suggestions relating to internet use, interviewing, information gathering, discussion and debate.

Historical Background

The Call of the 'Mother Country'

Over the centuries people from many countries have settled in Britain and contributed immensely to its history, prosperity, scientific and artistic achievements and cultural diversity. Following the end of World War II, because of labour shortages in some industries many young men and women were encouraged to seek new employment opportunities far from home. Britain had called on her subjects around the world to contribute to the war effort, and now was recruiting young men and women from the ex-colonies to help build the peace. Labour vouchers, professional training packages and other incentives were on offer, so that people who felt constrained by the shortage of opportunities available to them at home,

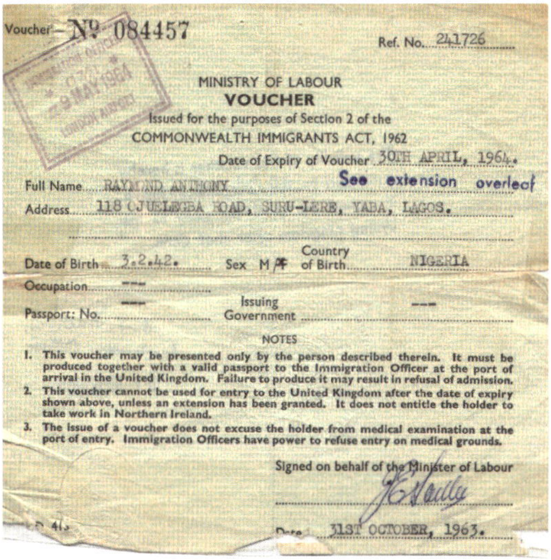
Voucher – Nº 084457 Ref. No. 241726

MINISTRY OF LABOUR
VOUCHER
Issued for the purposes of Section 2 of the
COMMONWEALTH IMMIGRANTS ACT, 1962

Date of Expiry of Voucher 30TH APRIL, 1964.

See extension overleaf

Full Name RAYMOND ANTHONY

Address 118 OJUELEGBA ROAD, SURU-LERE, YABA, LAGOS.

Date of Birth 3.2.42. Sex M Country of Birth NIGERIA

Occupation ---

Passport: No. --- Issuing Government ---

NOTES

1. This voucher may be presented only by the person described therein. It must be produced together with a valid passport to the Immigration Officer at the port of arrival in the United Kingdom. Failure to produce it may result in refusal of admission.
2. This voucher cannot be used for entry to the United Kingdom after the date of expiry shown above, unless an extension has been granted. It does not entitle the holder to take work in Northern Ireland.
3. The issue of a voucher does not excuse the holder from medical examination at the port of entry. Immigration Officers have power to refuse entry on medical grounds.

Signed on behalf of the Minister of Labour

Date 31ST OCTOBER, 1963.

took the chance to explore pastures new.

In most cases people expected to come to Britain for five years or less. Once they had generated enough money to improve the home situation, they planned to return and settle. However, although wages in general were usually higher in Britain than at home, immigrants often had to accept lower paid jobs, well below their real skill levels, on account of the prevailing racial prejudice. Living costs were higher too, so few people managed to save enough to return home in style and live there comfortably and permanently as they had anticipated.

New relationships provided another reason why many remained. The young men and women who came from the Caribbean, India and Africa in the post-war years sought the companionship of people from their home countries, often marrying people they met in Britain. Others were lonely and sent for girlfriends and wives from back home. Those who were already parents wished to improve their children's educational opportunities by having them grow up in Britain, and so saved and worked all hours so they could afford to bring the whole family here.

Many of these first generation immigrants have had to come to terms with their children associating closely with a host culture which is entirely different from, and in many ways threatening to their own. This shift in culture, and the underlying attitudes, has been further marked in the next generation, so the communication rift between grandparents and grandchildren is sometimes extreme. Many have not experienced the respectful treatment they expected and hoped for as elders. But most have adapted to life in Britain and made good lives over here, with family, friends, religious institutions and community centres to support them.

Elders Seeking Refuge

For some elders who arrived in Britain in the last quarter of the century as refugees fleeing civil wars and political upheaval in their own countries, life in Britain has been a tremendous struggle. Many such migrants have come to Britain later in their lives, when it is more difficult to adapt, and language skills are harder to acquire. For this reason, it is even more vital for these elders to be in touch with others who share similar backgrounds and languages.

Coming to Terms

Taking stock of their lives, as people often do in later years, throws up many conflicting feelings about the decisions they have made and the consequences reaped. This is particularly so for ethnic minority elders whose journeys have taken them so far from their starting point. Undertaking reminiscence in groups amongst people with similar or related experience can be a very helpful way of coming to terms with these feelings, as well as a way of providing mutual support and understanding. It can help to create a 'community of experience' with others who have made similar life journeys, so that people come to see their lives in a broader historical and social context.

One of many Caribbean NHS workers

A Cultural Legacy

Many elders who have been reflecting on the changes they have lived through, now wish to pass on the history and culture of their country of origin to the younger members of their families and communities. They can serve as 'time-witnesses' for their grandchildren and their friends, giving them a sense of their special heritage. We very much hope that the suggestions for inter-generational activities will help them to continue this important task of bearing witness, and preserving and transmitting their cultural heritage.

Geopolitical Backgrounds

CHINA & VIETNAM

By Helen Kon

Chinese people first settled in Britain around 1885. They were mainly seaman working on steamships and main settlements were in port cities of London, Cardiff and Liverpool.

Many Chinese who live in Britain today came in the 1960s from rural Hong Kong and set up takeaway food shops and other related business, while Chinese from Malaysia and Singapore came for further education and to obtain degrees. Others came from China, and Taiwan.

After the fall of Siagon in the summer of 1975, hundreds of thousands of Vietnamese began to flee the country in search of freedom and opportunities. Most of these Boat People were ethnic Chinese, who were facing fierce discrimination at home. They escaped in small wooden and unseaworthy boats across the South China Sea. They came upon the shores of neighbouring countries such as Hong Kong, Malaysia, Thailand, Indonesia, and Philippines where they entered the United Nations Refugee Camps. Some even made

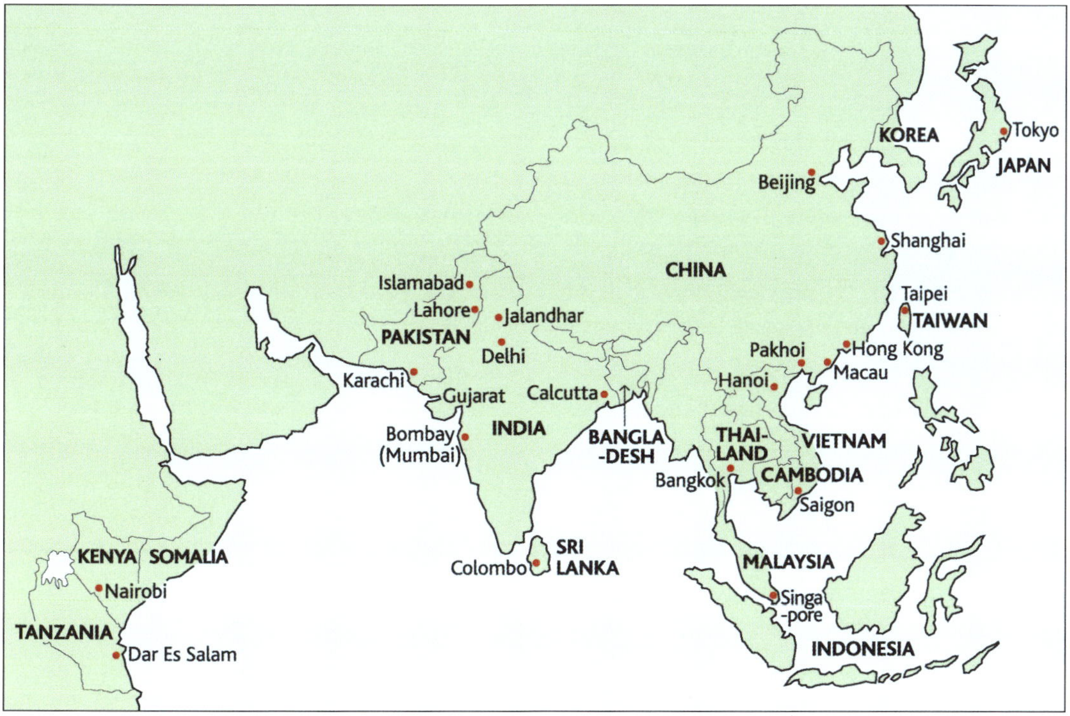

it to shores of South Korea and Japan. Most of these escapes had ended in tragedy. They had all endured perilous escapes to freedom that no-one could have imagined. Hundreds of thousands of unfortunate Vietnamese Boat People drowned in the unforgiving sea, died of hunger and dehydration or, tragically, were raped and killed by pirates. Some have estimated that more than a third of these escapees had died. Others escaped on foot across the border to China or Cambodia and then to Thailand .

A total of 214,555 refugees had reached the shores of Hong Kong. Life in the refugee camps was intolerable. The United Nations High Commissioner for Refugees and the Governor of Hong Kong appealed to governments around the world to admit some refugees. 22,000 Vietnamese were given asylum in the UK by 1990 from the agreed quotas and from family reunion.

The Government attempted to disperse them around the country, but this failed. About 14,000 re-grouped around Chinese communities in London. The most significant grouping of Vietnamese people in London is centred on six boroughs – Hackney, Tower Hamlets, Greenwich, Lewisham, Lambeth, and Southwark.

The Vietnamese who have settled are not from the same communities in Vietnam. They are from very different cultural, geographic and linguistic backgrounds. The majority are ethnic Chinese from North Vietnam. They speak Cantonese and a little Vietnamese, with the majority either Buddhists or Catholics. Most of the refugees were fisherman or farmers, although there were a small number of professionals.

Some Hong Kong Chinese were granted British passports as a result of the handover of Hong Kong to mainland China in 1997. These new immigrants are relatively better educated and have better professional skills.

INDIA

By Satya Devi Paul

The majority of Indians came to the United Kingdom in the 1960s. The Asians who came from India, Pakistan and what is now Bangladesh, came to work here in factories, London Transport, the National Health Service and in various trades, such as carpentry and engineering. Others were businessmen and professionals. The menfolk came first, often living in crowded conditions and working all hours to raise enough money to send home to their families and to save for a home in Britain to bring their wives and children over.

There were many East African Asians who had settled in Kenya, Tanzania and Uganda. Their situation as an ethnic minority was increasingly uncomfortable when these countries became independent in the early 1960s. This was especially so for the Ugandan Asians living under Idi Amin, who eventually forced them all to leave in 1972, giving them only two weeks' notice to get out. They were British subjects and passport holders, so they came to Britain with their families. Most of these people had been business men and professionals in East Africa, who led comfortable lives, but they had had to leave almost everything behind, including servants, money and possessions. When they came to Britain, they set up businesses and opened corner shops or made their way in the medical profession.

Asians settling in Britain in the 1960s and 70s were mainly Sikhs or Muslims, with Punjabi or Gujerati backgrounds. Those coming from Bangladesh, a little later were mainly Muslims. Many had worked on ships and as labourers or cooks and they set up restaurants all over the country. In the 1980s, Asian families who had settled in Britain in the 1960s and 70s were feeling the pull of family obligations and worrying about ailing parents back home, so many brought their elderly parents over to join them. All these groups now have their own places of worship, temples and mosques, and community centres where traditional food and cultural activities are provided, often on a voluntary basis.

NIGERIA

By Ade Aderogba

Nigeria is a West African country with a population of about 120 million, the largest of all African countries. The country was a British colony until 1960 when it became independent and it is now a member of the Commonwealth.

Nigeria is a developing country with serious economic challenges including high unemployment leading to considerable pressure to migrate. It is a country of contradictions because there are pockets of great wealth amidst severe poverty. It is the largest oil producing country in Africa and has the third largest natural gas reserves in the world.

In the 1950s and 60s many bright students who had been to British-run secondary schools came to the UK to study planning to return to Nigeria to run the country after independence. It was known as the Nigerianisation Policy. There were British government-funded bursaries and awards to help provide the academic brains that would run the largest black country on earth. The overwhelming majority of such students returned home and did just this. Those who are living in Britain today who came over in that period have come back due to inter-racial marriages and similar circumstances, but most of these people too have maintained links with Nigeria and return there from time to time.

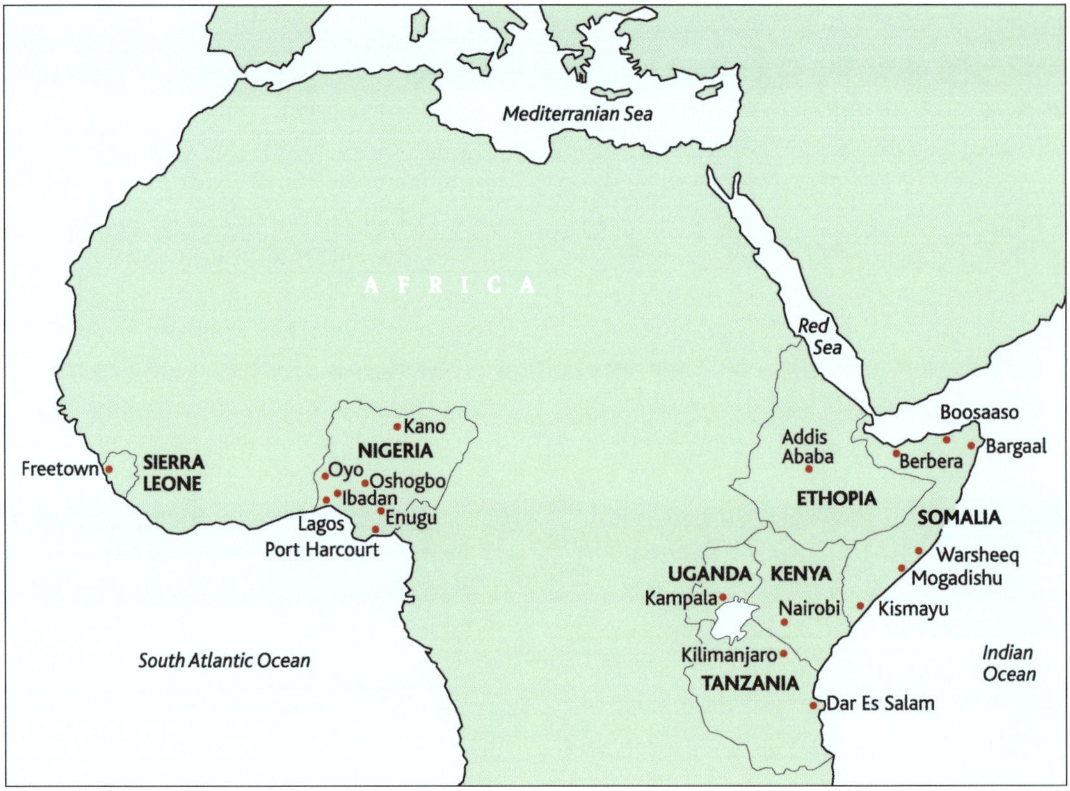

There are about 250 different languages or tribal groups but the dominant ones are the Yorubas in the south west, the Hausas in the north and the Igbos in the south eastern areas. Oil was discovered in the south east around 1958 and after independence in 1960 there was some temptation for the south eastern leaders to secede from the Federation and become an oil-rich nation. There was a military coup in January 1966 when the Prime Minister Tafawa Balewa was assassinated. This led to a civil war between 1967 – 1970 when Colonel Odumegwu Ojukwu the Igbo leader declared his territory as independent of Nigeria, naming it 'Biafra'.

Over one million people died as a result of the war, but the country is now fully reunited under an elected system of government. Olusegun Obasanjo, a Yoruba, is the President. The military have ruled Nigeria for most of its independence but the people now seem to prefer a democratic system and voter turnouts are usually very high.

SOMALIA

By Zeinab Mahmood

In the late nineteenth century, European powers carved up the African continent. The British, Italians and French ruled over the Somali people, frequently invading each other's colonial territories. Somalia did not achieve independence until 1960.

Almost all Somalis speak the same language and belong to the same ethnic group, and for a decade after independence there was a relatively stable parliamentary democracy. But clans, often armed and trained by the major powers, vied with one another to form their own political parties. In 1969, General Siad Barre seized power in a military coup. He undertook to break the clan system and modernise the country and at first he was very popular, but he brutally suppressed all opposition and unleashed a reign of terror and intimidation on his people. He tried to regain popularity at home by invading neighbouring Ethiopia in 1974 when Emperor Haile Sellassie fell, but this venture was a disaster.

Somalia was left a very poor country. It had fallen into debt in the late 1970s and the International Monetary Fund forced the government to reduce its spending. Food subsidies were cut, causing hardship in the towns particularly. The 1980s saw a huge refugee crisis, following continued border conflict with Ethiopia and widespread famine, and by 1992 over four million Somalis were at risk of starvation. During 1992 over 500,000 died as a result of fighting between different militias and starvation, including many thousands of children under five years old. An international Task Force and many aid agencies tried to help through Operation Restore Hope, but they were constantly hampered by the rival militias to whom they had to pay protection money in order to get food through to the people. They saved thousands of lives, but did not manage to disarm the militias before withdrawing their forces.

Many of the Somalis who have sought refuge in Britain have lost family members in the last years and many still have relatives living in Somalia whom they would like to bring to safety. Most older Somalis living in Britain hope to return home when their country is once more at peace.

SIERRA LEONE

By Belmont Williams

Sierra Leone is one of the smallest countries in Africa. The United Nations estimated the population in the 1990s as 4.428 million, but it must be much lower than this after the civil war that lasted ten years. There are about twenty African tribes in the country. The largest are the Mendes in the South and East and the Temnes in the North. The Krios live predominantly in Freetown and the Western

Area and they constitute only about ten percent of the population. The language of the Krios is called Creole. It is a language developed over about 100 years and became the lingua franca of the country. The Krios are the descendants of freed slaves. In early 1808 the country became a British Crown Colony and in 1896 Britain established a Protectorate that covered the greater part of the country outside Freetown. Sierra Leone became independent in 1961 and the Protectorate was subsequently renamed the Provinces. As far as religion is concerned, Christianity is the religion of only about 10 percent of the population; Islam accounts for just over half of the population and the rest have traditional beliefs.

Sierra Leone used to be a peaceful and beautiful country. It is richly endowed with mineral resources such as diamonds, the major root cause of our problems, gold, bauxite and rutile, the last two being minerals which are important in industrial production. Fish is plentiful and the soil is fertile everywhere. Unfortunately,as a result of corruption, greed and misrule, the country was thrown into a state of anarchy and a war that went on for ten years with considerable destruction of life and property. It is hard to imagine the appaling atrocities that were committed. For a country with such potential to be ranked now as the least developed country in the world according to United Nations assessment, and heavily dependent on handouts, has left many of us frustrated, baffled, disappointed and helpless.

Most of the Sierra Leoneans who left the country in the 1950s did so to study at various British universities and colleges or to undergo vocational training. The Principals of most of the Secondary schools, until the country became independent, were British, and many scholarships were awarded to Sierra Leoneans to study in Britain. Most returned home on completion of their studies to help prepare for independence and take up leadership posts.

Britain has made a considerable contribution to Sierra Leone, especially in the creation of the Civil Service, the health sector and the Judiciary. In the commercial sector, Britain contributed to establishing banks and trading houses.

THE CARIBBEAN

By Arthur Torrington

The original inhabitants of the Caribbean were the Arawak and Carib Indians. Most of them were killed by British, French, Spanish and Portuguese settlers in the 17th and 18th centuries. For the past four hundred years, the United Kingdom has played an integral part in the lives of Caribbean people. African slaves were first taken in ships to the Caribbean islands in the 1600s, and the income from the plantations helped to make Britain great. Cut

off from their homelands, the slaves developed a new way of life with European and Indian influences.

There were more than seventeen British colonies in the West Indies, including British Guiana (now Guyana) and British Honduras (now Belize) which are on the mainland of South and Central America. The total population is now under ten million.

Since the 17th century, millions of Britons have emigrated to the New World. But large-scale emigration from the Caribbean to the UK did not take place until 21 June 1948 when a ship 'Empire Windrush' landed at Tilbury Docks, Essex. On board were more than 500 Caribbean people, most of whom were ex-servicemen and women who had fought for this country in the Second World War.

When the Windrush pioneers arrived, many of them lived in the Clapham South Deep Shelter, where a few years before, the people of South London had to go to shelter from German bombs. But during that summer the settlers found homes in Brixton, Balham, Wandsworth, Lewisham, Greenwich, and other parts of London.

That was the beginning of the Black community, as we know it today.

Over the years, thousands of Caribbean settlers arrived to help rebuild Britain. Many rejoined the Royal Air Force; some worked in the National Health Service, transport, central and local government, the building trade, and other occupations. Those early pioneers are now senior citizens, who have made a significant contribution to the country's prosperity. They were the ones who brought Caribbean culture to Britain. The popularity of Reggae music and the Notting Hill carnival is due to the foundation the Windrush generation has laid.

About Reminiscence Work

By Pam Schweitzer

Reminiscence is the act or process of recalling and sharing one's memories, and is a normal part of everyday life for most people of all ages. In their later years, however, people often lose those with whom they have most in common, whether through bereavement or geographical separation, leaving them feeling very alone with their memories. It can therefore be very enjoyable and helpful to join in more structured reminiscence sessions. These may be one-to-one sessions with another person for the specific purpose of retracing, reviewing and reflecting back over a lifetime's experience in order to achieve a sense of completeness and resolution. More commonly it will involve joining a group with others of a similar age and background to share memories and to make new friendships and connections.

A group leader or facilitator will stimulate and guide the discussion, introduce exercises and activities and will frequently use multi-sensory triggers to stimulate the return and reconsideration of memories. Most of the exercises and creative activities suggestions attached to each chapter of this book relate to group work, but the same underlying principles inform all reminiscence.

Over the last twenty-five years, there has been a considerable growth in reminiscence activity with older people. Its benefits in terms of health and social well-being have become more and more valued.

SOME REASONS FOR DOING REMINISCENCE WORK

Community Building

Sharing memories with others from a similar background generates a strong sense of belonging to a community and having a valued role within it.

Cultural Integration

Reminiscence is also a means of celebrating difference, bringing communities with different racial, cultural and religious backgrounds together to exchange life experience.

Combating Isolation

Loss of partners and close friends in later life can lead to isolation and withdrawal. Reminiscence offers a means of inclusion in a desirable social group which shares a common life experience.

Friendship

Pleasurable contact through sharing common memories can become the basis for new friendships between participants in the present.

Finding Perspective
Having an opportunity to share and reflect on one's experience of life in a supportive atmosphere increases people's sense of identity, their sense of who they are. It helps people to integrate the different parts of their life into a more meaningful whole.

A Sense of History
Sharing stories with people of the same generation or with much younger people helps to develop a sense of oneself as a participant in the great social and historical upheavals of the last century.

Respect
Everyone is the expert on his or her own life and is recognised as an individual with unique experience to impart.

Stimulation
Being in a group where the memories are held in common and shared can stimulate the recall of long-forgotten experiences and put participants back in touch with parts of their lives which are pleasurable to remember.

Psychological Support
Where memories are painful, it can be

helpful to find others who can relate to one's own past struggles, so one does not have to feel so alone in suffering.

Creativity
Encouraging people to explore their memories through creative activities is pleasurable for participants and entertaining for anyone with whom they may wish to share their results.

Empowerment
Reminiscence work with people with special needs, and especially older people with dementia, can help to build self-confidence and independence by concentrating on strengths and creating opportunities for success.

ESSENTIAL REMINISCENCE SKILLS AND QUALITIES

Readers who wish to undertake this work for the first time might like to reflect on the essential elements of the reminiscence process and the skills and qualities it requires. Some of the essential skills listed below may sound so obvious that they don't need pointing out. It is true that some people are 'naturals' when it comes to engaging with older people and valuing their memories, but it is necessary to practise and develop these essential skills to use them purposely and in a planned way.

Good Listening Skills
Be very attentive to what each speaker is saying, showing that you are 'there' for them, and do not rush to prompt or question.

Receptiveness
Relax, and show in your body language, including eye contact, that you are pleased to be listening and that you are interested and value what is being said.

Curiosity
You need to have a genuine desire to know more and to learn from the older people, especially as they will be very quick to stop reminiscing if they feel you are bored or doing this work out of duty.

Sensitivity
Make yourself receptive to the feelings which the speaker is revealing as well as the content, especially where a painful memory may have been triggered, and guard against questioning which may be experienced as intrusive.

An Accepting Attitude
Do not judge the person remembering, but rather show that you have heard and understood what they said and respect their point of view.

A Reasonable Memory
You must be able to recall what has been said and be able to refer back to it, in order

to make the person remembering feel it is worthwhile talking to you, and so you can make links between different stories.

A Sense of Humour

You need be able to create an easy atmosphere, sharing the funny side of things remembered, and delighting in the unexpected and bizarre.

Adaptability

You must be willing to change plans quickly and 'go with' the interests and needs expressed by the person, or the group, without making them feel that you have no sense of direction yourself.

Imagination

Some people find that talking is more difficult than other means of communication, such as drawing, singing, dancing, showing, etc, so you need to provide many possibilities for creative expression of memories.

ADDITIONAL REQUIREMENTS WHEN WORKING WITH A GROUP

Clarity

Be clear about the group's purpose and objectives, make sure people know and accept them, including practical aspects such as the number and duration of sessions, where they will be held and when.

A Democratic Approach

Everyone's contributions must be valued and the time available to the group must be shared.

Confidentiality

It is essential to create a sense of security and confidentiality within the group and to make sure all group members accept this idea.

Group Work Skills

There are always links and connections between what different group members say, however different their backgrounds may be. Good facilitation involves pointing up these links for the group and creating a sense of shared experience and common ground.

Preparedness

Group work needs forward planning so that culturally appropriate resources are to hand which will stimulate all the senses. This includes having relevant things to taste, smell, handle, look at, listen to and use in the sessions.

Confidence

The group must feel that the facilitator knows what he or she is doing, and can take control if difficult situations arise between people in the group or around painful or challenging memories.

Courage
The group leader should be willing to tackle complex and emotional subjects, as long as the group wishes. S/he must not lose confidence if there are moments of sadness, bearing in mind that the empathy and support of other group members who have shared similar experiences is one of the elements that can make reminiscence such a comforting process.

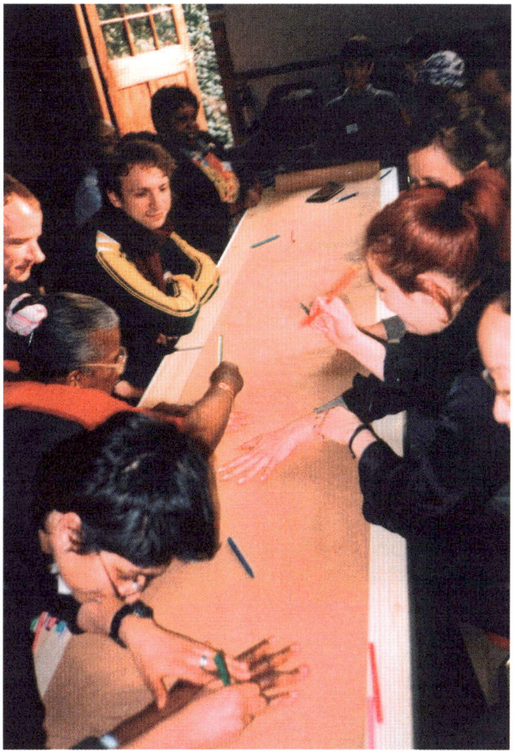

Caring
There is a responsibility to take care of the emotional needs of group members, ensuring that each person is welcomed individually. If someone is distressed, time should be made for them to talk (if necessary after the session) and extra help should be made available if required.

Practicality
The physical needs of the group must be considered, so that everyone can hear and see everyone else in the session. Arrangements should be made for people who are hard of hearing to sit near or opposite the group leader, and the room should be quiet, warm, well-lit and undisturbed.

Care Staff
Wherever possible, it is desirable to include in the reminiscence sessions care staff, volunteers and any others who may be looking after the group members. Through joining in the sessions, they can learn more about the backgrounds, likes and dislikes, achievements, skills, joys and sorrows of the older people. This knowledge can make a significant difference to their job satisfaction, by increasing their understanding, providing topics for future conversation and assisting them to care for the elders in a more personal way.

PLANNING A SERIES OF REMINISCENCE SESSIONS

Agreeing structure, ground rules length, time and place
The chapters in this book offer a chrono-

Born in the Caribbean Resource Box

logical approach to structuring reminiscence work, but of course there are many other alternatives. For example, one can follow the cycle of the current year, and ask the group to share memories associated with different seasons and festivals. Or one can pick themes that are of interest to each member of the group in turn, and jump backwards and forwards in time.

Another approach is to concentrate on one subject or theme over a number of weeks, exploring it ever more deeply, with a group who have a real interest in it.

Having a particular end-product in mind from the outset, whether it be a play, a film, a book or an exhibition of photos and memories, will also provide a framework for the sessions. Begin with gathering memories, and then go on to either recording and editing them or exploring them through expressive and visual arts until the material is ready for presenting to others. In any of these instances, it is desirable to have all members sign a simple form at the beginning of the process, indicating that they are happy to have their material used for educational, research or performance purposes.

Whatever the proposed plan , it is important for the participants to understand it, accept it in outline, and feel able to contribute to shaping it as it develops. There does not need to be any written contract with the group, but it is necessary to agree about objectives and ground rules at the outset, especially concerning mutual respect and confidentiality, attentive listening to one another, and a willingness to share memories in a non-judgemental atmosphere.

The group leader needs to agree a framework for the reminiscence sessions, saying how many weeks the group will run and roughly what theme or topic will be discussed in which week. However, it is very important to be flexible enough to respond to spontaneous developments within the group. A great interest in a particular topic, for example, may emerge and it might therefore need two weeks to itself, or an event in the external world might trigger a lot of memories which need to be shared in the group.

Each session needs to have a shape, with starter activities, a main section for story-telling and creative work, and a conclusion, which should include a summary of what has been covered and confirmation of what will be talked about in the next session. It is desirable to build a break for refreshments into each session, as this can strengthen the group feeling and create a relaxed atmosphere.

There needs to be a balance between the safety of trusting the group leader and the excitement of feeling that anything can happen and that the group members themselves can be instrumental in making it happen. The group leader needs to remind the group how many sessions remain, and alert them to the approaching end, preparing a final session which celebrates what they have achieved. If the group members really wish to continue after the proposed number of sessions has been completed, it is important that the leader renegotiates with them and agrees a new schedule. It is always safer for the leader and the group to commit to a fixed number of sessions (between six and twelve) and then extend, rather than start with long-term commitments that have to be shortened.

Themes and Topics

Some themes are particularly fruitful to explore with groups, and many activities attached to the chapters that follow focus on these themes:

- Childhood games and pastimes
- Family life and grandparents
- Food and cooking
- School days
- Ambitions and dreams
- Starting work
- Courting days
- Entertainment and fashion
- Weddings

- Having babies and bringing up a family
- Festivals, rituals, special occasions, weekends
- Significant journeys, holidays and travel
- Wartime memories (but this is not appropriate for everyone)

Multi-Sensory Triggers

Whatever the theme, it is important to offer different types of sensory stimulation in order to help people remember. Objects familiar to group members from earlier days are a good starting point and they can stimulate many senses. For example, an old hand-made shopping basket will have a smell, a texture, a design, a weight when empty and full, a physical association with carrying and shopping, and a taste connection with food purchased in the past in markets and shops. Objects also have different associations for different people, so that comparing one person's memory of going shopping with someone else's will be a way of conjuring up their different backgrounds and communities.

Often objects provide a more relaxing starting point than questions, provided

they are chosen with care and are culturally appropriate to the group members. Here are some of the sources of stimulation which can help to make reminiscence sessions varied and enjoyable:

Sight
Photos, films, paintings and colours, maps, flags and symbols, diagrams, technical drawings, posters, skies, growing things.

Sounds
Songs, familiar and unfamiliar music, bird and animal sounds, weather (storms, wind, rain), sounds of trains and ships, machinery noise.

Words
Place names, famous people, stories, scandals, proverbs and poems.

Tastes
Food, drink, sweets, medicine, cooking and baking, unusual or foreign foods to try, old recipes remembered from childhood.

Smells
Medicine, perfume, make-up, cleaning agents, mothballs, herbs, spices, cooking smells, flowers, trees and countryside smells, coal and wood burning.

Touch
Contrasting textures, contrasting temperatures (warm and cold), different fabrics, human touch, food ingredients, animals to stroke, babies to cuddle, clothes to handle and fold.

Movement
Games, dance, mime, greetings, gestures, work movements such as typing, sewing, lifting, digging, religious rituals.

GROUP REMINISCENCE WORK WITH ETHNIC MINORITY ELDERS

Intercultural work
Not all elders find themselves spending their later years in the company of people who share their language and culture, especially if their work or their family attachments have involved them in moving away from London, Birmingham or one of the other big cities. They are likely to be sharing a day centre or sheltered house or club room with old people born in Britain, or coming from many different parts of the world. Reminiscence can be very beneficial as a means of bringing out the things these old people have in common with their neighbours, and enjoying some of the special and different stories of their own lives. Group sessions can be a means of opening up communication, creating understanding between people from different cultures in the present and stimulating all concerned.

Working Through Interpreters

Where elders do not share a language with the people they are living with, this can lead to feelings of isolation and alienation. One of the Chinese story-tellers in this book discovered this, living as the only 'foreigner' in a sheltered housing complex in Kent, where he moved to be near his son. In this situation, the reminiscence group leader will need to make special arrangements for translation, so that elders from minorities can be included and there can be an inter-cultural exchange in the group.

Some Places to Start Looking for Help with Translation

The obvious place to start is with the family of the person concerned, in case there is a child or grandchild living close enough to come in for these sessions. This has the great benefit of enabling the younger relative to discover more about their own history and to be of service in helping the older person settle into the group and find their place.

An advertisement in the local press may attract someone in the area who speaks the relevant language and who would be willing to help on a voluntary basis or for a small fee.

Social services departments and health authorities offer translation services and may be able to help as an extension to their existing services or know of a volunteer or family member they have called on in the past.

A local language school may have attracted students from the home country of the elder concerned and they might be willing to help over an eight week period during their visit to Britain. This would be helpful for the group leader and give an extra sense of purpose for the student.

The local college or university may have students with the relevant language who may be pleased to offer a couple of hours a week on a fixed term basis as part of their community service. A small payment may be necessary, but the benefits would be considerable to the older person, the group leader and particularly to the student. A local employment agency may know of suitable candidates.

Make sure that any interpreter involved in a reminiscence session has an idea of the purpose of the group, and really translates everything the older person actually says. This may sound obvious, but some interpreters are more used to obtaining factual information, and may not be clear about the need to translate the feelings, doubts, regrets and joys which are linked to those facts. If they become part of the session and see how the group leader is offering openings for self-expression and creativity to the elders, they will want to give much fuller translations.

Preparation and Background Reading

The reminiscence group leader who wishes to include people from different backgrounds in their sessions should prepare a little. It is not necessary to spend a great deal of time reading around and researching, but it is helpful to have some background to draw on to encourage conversation if the older person needs prompting. It is reassuring too for the elders if they gather that the group leader is genuinely interested in them and their background. Given this support and encouragement, the older people themselves can be the guides to their own country, its recent history and its culture.

Some Practical Ways for Group Leaders to Prepare

Find a map (through the local library or from the internet) which locates the home country of the elder in relation to the rest of the world. Is it an island or part of a mainland? Is it mountainous or flat? What is the nearest big city or landmark which some of the rest of the group might know?

If possible find images of the home country, again either through the local library or on the internet, so the elder has a starting point and the other group members can form a clearer picture of the person's homeland and their journey.

Find out a little about the history of the country. Does it have historical ties

with Britain through a colonial past? Or was there a conflict in the home country that led to the older person seeking refuge in Britain? This does not need to be very detailed information, but enough for the group leader to be able to deal sensitively with issues which may crop up in the group.

Check the religious background of the individuals involved, and find out the key beliefs, observances and festivals of that religion. When discussing childhood and marriage in reminiscence groups, these subjects are likely to arise, but they can also offer a starting point for a reminiscence session. Again, this knowledge will be helpful in finding common threads, such as festivals of light in the winter months and harvest festivals when the crops are ready.

Try to find a couple of objects which are specific to the culture of the person you wish to introduce to the group, so there is a starting point. This could be through a local market or museum, or through a cultural centre in the area. It could even be a fruit or vegetable which is grown and cooked in that country. Maybe the older person will have something themselves, an object or photo from their homeland or from their early days in Britain, which has a story attached to it.

Try to have some one-to-one communication with the older person before working with the group. Visiting the person in his or her present home environment is often the quickest and most fruitful way of finding triggers for reminiscence, but this may not be possible. In any case, if there is some connection and relationship established it will ease introduction to the group and help to create confidence and trust all round.

Same Language Groups

Even in a group where all the members share a faith or a language, it is likely that they will come from many different regions and very varied social and educational backgrounds. They will have many stories to tell one another about their lives back home and their experience of settling in Britain. The reminiscence process highlights the uniqueness of each member's experience and generates mutual interest and appreciation. There will also be knowledge and experience in common, and group leaders can call on this to develop feelings of group solidarity.

Singing and dancing together to the music of the home country is an obvious bonding activity, just as it is in any other reminiscence group, but with the added power of bringing a remembered faraway place alive in a very different present. Reminiscence sessions that include the preparation and sharing of traditional foods can be particularly successful, as smells and tastes are powerful means of evoking memories. Asking some group members to bring along their traditional costumes can stimulate discussion about the important people and occasions in each person's life and about the special designs and fabrics associated with the places where they grew up. In the activities sections of each chapter there are suggestions for specific activities to explore where people have come from, the major journeys in their lives and the adjustments they have made.

Some reminiscence sessions should have a quieter atmosphere, with people sharing memories with just one other person in a confidential way, sympathising with and understanding one another's more painful feelings and memories. They can then decide, perhaps selectively, to share what they have been remembering with the whole group, and begin to explore their stories creatively together. However, it is important to remind people that it is up to them to decide what to share, and that personal privacy will be respected.

At the end of a session of exchanging memories, people should feel that they have expressed what they have in common and acknowledged each individual in the group. "What a special and interesting collection of people we are!" is a common response to a lively session, and that is why reminiscence can develop people's personal confidence and increase their sense of belonging.

Dealing With Painful Issues

Reminiscence sessions often lead into more wide-ranging discussions concerning how people's past decisions are now affecting their lives, often in ways they had not wished or expected. Feelings of pain, displacement and loss will surface, anxieties concerning citizenship and security, fears for health and welfare in the future, and unresolved family problems and conflicts. Fear of raising these issues can inhibit workers who may wish to undertake reminiscence work. They may feel that they are not adequately prepared to deal with the 'fall-out' from such discussions and that it is safer to avoid them. However, reminiscence sessions can provide a valuable opportunity for group members to share some of these painful feelings with others who are familiar with them and who can empathise. This sharing often helps to reduce the burden for the elders of coping with such feelings alone and provides much-needed support for individuals. In this sense, reminiscence is not just about sharing the past, but very much about coping with the present and facing the future.

Recording Memories

One of the main motivators for ethnic minority elders is the desire to pass on their own culture and life experience to younger people from their own ethnic background. It is therefore important to offer this possibility to elders who express an interest in reminiscence, as well as providing them with the pleasurable opportunity of talking to others of their own generation.

If a reminiscence group is being recorded, it is important to ask people to speak one at a time, and to say their names before speaking. This avoids a lot of confusion for the person transcribing the tape, but it also creates the right atmosphere of respectful listening which is essential if the speaker is going to feel that the effort is worthwhile. People must be asked if they are content to have the session recorded, and the reasons for doing so should be explained. No individual should be obliged to speak or made to feel bad if they decide just to listen.

The most common method is to record what people say in the group on to a tape machine or minidisk and then write out some of the most interesting stories. It is desirable to stick closely to the speech patterns of the story-teller, but always make sure a reader can easily grasp what the speaker meant, tidying and clarifying where necessary and omitting statements

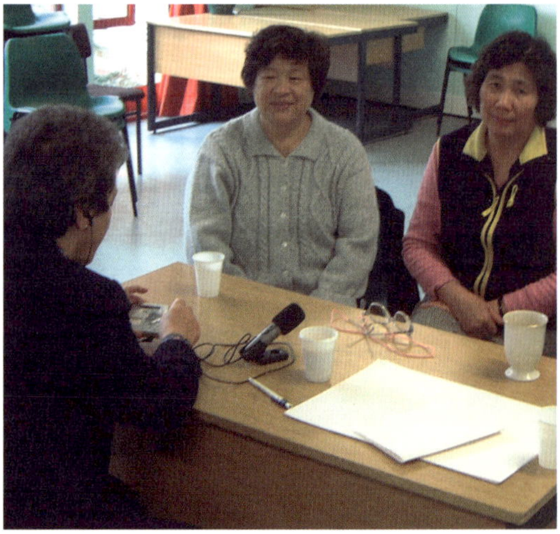

which are muddled or confusing.

Transcribing recorded memories is a time-consuming process, but it is a very effective way of showing group members that what they say is valuable and valued. It is desirable to put in at least a sentence from each person in any such summary, so that no one feels left out or inadequate. It helps everyone to feel part of a significant process and starts them imagining who else might be interested to read these memories.

If the text is typed and enlarged, the story can be exhibited on the walls of the meeting place to show others using the building what is going on in the group, and what interesting stories the elders have to tell. Photos of the group at work, perhaps showing some of the objects they have brought into the group, will help to get the message across.

Using video to record reminiscence sessions is now much easier than before, since cameras are tiny and so unobtrusive that they do not inhibit the speakers, but always ask for the group's consent before filming. Video is a good medium for capturing and remembering the spirit of a group in action. It can be enjoyable for a group to watch themselves on film and remember what fun they had together, and recall some of the stories they may have forgotten from previous sessions. It is also useful to film people's old photographs and objects. These images can be used with voice-over commentary in any future edited version. However, video editing is skilled work and can be expensive, so unless this element is funded, the tapes may have a limited value, except as a record of the group in action.

One other use of video tape is as a training and consciousness-raising tool for the reminiscence group leader, and any volunteers or co-workers who may be involved in the sessions. It can illustrate skilled leadership and assist people to identify lost opportunities, inept or insensitive responses and draw attention to the need to include, rather than exclude, all members. For this sort of use, it is sensible to film sparingly from time to time during a session, so that there is not hours of footage produced which no one will have the time to watch.

Creative Development of the Memories

It often happens that people who start to record their stories become much more confident and outward-looking as a consequence. They might well start wondering how can they further explore their own creativity as a group, and who else would be interested in what they have to say and show. A natural development from the sessions is to make a small exhibition which others can enjoy and which will demonstrate the life of the group. The exhibition could include memories, photos (both past and present), drawings produced during the sessions and perhaps some objects that the elders have brought in to share with the group. Some people may worry about their more personal experiences being shown publicly and it is important to let them decide on any cuts or edits. Creating an exhibition together is enjoyable and can develop the group's confidence and sense of achievement.

Another means of sharing the reminiscence work with others is to develop a short entertainment of stories and songs recalled by the group during the sessions. The programme may need a compère or link person to prompt the performers, and this could be the reminiscence group leader or another group member. It can include some solo pieces for confident members and some songs to perform all together. Again, the individual members must feel comfortable with what they are sharing, and must have the right to cut out a story which leaves them feeling exposed in an uncomfortable way. Preparing an event of this kind is another way of strengthening positive feelings about the group and offering an opportunity for sharing with a wider audience.

Some groups enjoy making improvised scenes from the stories they have told, and these can be threaded together into an informal piece of theatre to share with others. This approach is becoming more popular as groups realise what fun this can be, and that no previous acting experience is required. The scenes can remain improvised, so that people do not get nervous about learning lines and so that the spontaneity of the performance is preserved. There is scope for comedy here, and also for moments of sadness as people convey more complex memories. Songs can be interspersed to help the group move easily from one scene and one mood to another.

The video which accompanies this book shows examples of all these approaches. It was filmed during a period when groups of ethnic minority elders in the London Borough of Greenwich were preparing for a festival of reminiscence arts and many of the groups were using these creative approaches to reminiscence for the first time. Working towards a festival for inter-cultural sharing of memories can be an excellent way of galvanising the energy of the groups concerned. It can enable them to focus on what is important to them to transmit to others who may be from different cultures or different generations. The process of preparation must not be too pressured, and it should not become a competition between the groups. As long as the spirit behind the event is one of co-operation and celebration, a festival can be an ideal means of generating creative reminiscence work that will improve the quality of life for participants.

REMINISCENCE WORK ACROSS THE GENERATIONS

Sharing stories from different cultures with children from different racial backgrounds in a classroom can be a powerful way of creating inter-cultural and intergenerational understanding. It is very important in such meetings that the older person is well prepared and supported, and that the teacher has done some background work with the children and created a respectful atmosphere.

Old and young Caribbeans work together on a dramatisation of leaving home

Passing memories across generations and cultures

There are many benefits to both generations. Older people enjoy the energy, enthusiasm and playfulness of children, and often reconnect with these qualities in themselves. Elders who visit classrooms to talk about when they were young, often find they can remember the songs and dances of their childhood and pass these on to today's children. They are often surprised themselves at how their lives are so interesting to children in schools, especially if their own schooldays were not marked by success, and they can become more confident as a result. When teachers and children use these inter-generational encounters as a basis for creative work in the classroom, the resulting displays of art, drama and creative writing are extremely gratifying for the older people involved, who feel that their lives are being recognised and celebrated.

For younger people it often comes as a revelation that the older people in front of them were once young like them, but in a different world. They soon recognise that there is much more to older people than just what you can see in the present and treat the elders with much more respect as a result. Young people's understanding of life in the past, and the changes that have occurred, can be deepened by listening to the first hand testimony of older people. These accounts can be verified and expanded through curriculum work in geography and history, including information searches through libraries and from the internet.

There can be further educational, social and cultural benefits when the stories of these 'time witnesses' are explored in the classroom through drama, art and creative writing. These creative approaches help the children to relate what they have heard to their own experience of life, and make greater sense of it.

For children and grandchildren of immigrants, a sense of personal and community history is especially important in building self-esteem. Older people have a very positive role to play here, re-enforcing a cultural legacy, passing on personal stories and customs, and stimulating children in their communities to be interested in their own families' histories. By making bridges between generations and cultures in the classroom, ethnic minority elders can play their part in increasing social cohesion and understanding.

It is important that all our children have some understanding of why Britain is a multicultural society today. When older people from the Caribbean, for example, explain to children how they came in the post-war years to work in nursing or public transport or heavy industry when the 'mother country' was crying out for help, it assists children to understand the bigger changes in society and how they are affected by them. They can see history as something that happens to 'ordinary' people as well as great leaders, and indeed that it is 'ordinary' people who can make change and change history.

Other countries' recent histories are different from ours, but are significant for us, and need to be reflected in curriculum work. We hope the stories in this book, and the suggestions for exploring them through creative activities, will be of help to teachers and students alike.

Much has changed in the way schools study history, geography, society and religions, especially in urban multicultural classrooms. There is now a great deal more acknowledgement of diversity, and of the educational value of accepting difference as a means of combating racism. The richness and variety of the pupils' family backgrounds are increasingly being recognised as a resource that cannot be overlooked. The grandparents and great grandparents of the children have important stories to tell.

An Introduction to the Stories

By Meena Khatwa

This book is the result of a project which ran from January 2003 to January 2004. It was funded by the Community Fund, and worked in partnership with Greenwich Council for Racial Equality and Greenwich Arts and Culture Office. I was employed by Age Exchange to co-ordinate the project with my colleague Indie Choudhury as Project Administrator. Our aim was to deliver a very exciting, ambitious and richly developed resource of black and ethnic elders' memories.

The project focused on interviewing elders within the borough of Greenwich. Our starting point was to carry out extensive outreach with the African, Caribbean, Asian, Chinese and Vietnamese communities.

The first four months of the project were spent networking with housing schemes, day centres and luncheon clubs. We were new to the area, and strangers to the groups, so it was important to make good connections with them and build up trust. This we did, with the invaluable support of Satya Devi Paul, the Ethnic Elders Officer at Greenwich Council for Racial Equality. The commitment and enthusiasm shared by the managers and community leaders such as Helen Kon, Aimee Soodoo, Nassim Khodabux, Joan Scantlebury and Atia Malik played a crucial role in the successful engagement of all participants. Part of the remit of the project was to organise forums for all the community leaders and managers and to provide training in reminiscence and creative activities. From the outset we aimed to involve the leaders in the process, development and delivery of the project.

The first months of the project, highlighted many important issues which were vital to its successful development. We realised that we couldn't just walk in and expect individuals or groups to volunteer their life stories or eagerly participate in reminiscence sessions. It became apparent that many were not aware of what reminiscence was or what it could do for them.

Regardless of their backgrounds, we heard the same concerns from the older people: "Why do you want to interview me?" "My life isn't interesting" "Who would want to hear about my stories?" Naturally the elderly groups were cautious and it became clear that we had to spend time with them before they could feel confident about sharing their memories and proud of their experiences. We shared our feelings and reasons why their stories needed to be heard and how a legacy should remain of their hopes and struggles. Furthermore their stories could be educational, challenge ignorance about different cultures and raise awareness about how these communities lived in their native homes. Their experiences were in danger of being lost forever, but they could now be shared with future generations who may not have a close relationship with their grandparents or older people in their communities.

We gradually became familiar faces at the centres and the sheltered housing schemes and the groups began to look forward to the reminiscence sessions. As a result of the time and effort put in, individuals began to come forward. The interviews took place in different spaces and with groups as well as individuals. It was wonderful to see how the storytellers shared all types of emotions when being transported back to their past lives and their childhood homes. There were many sharply remembered details and descriptions of fascinating rituals, customs and events which were recalled through gestures, actions or replaying their memories. There was a genuine sense of contentment, excitement and at times feelings of sorrow in what was being revealed. At times, as the interviewer, I felt as though I had travelled the world without ever leaving the borough of Greenwich.

During the year it was interesting to see how a deeply-buried sense of value had returned to these elders' memories. This growing confidence has also been the

result of close working relationships between the elders and the project arts workers who have developed and produced drama and artwork pieces based on their memories.

Looking back over the year, I have learned much more about my own community as well as the Chinese, African and Caribbean elders. I have been made aware of the struggles and harsh reality that many elders face, and how there has been a shift in the cultural and traditional structure of the extended family. As a second generation Asian, I have felt fortunate to have grown up with my grandparents and learned about customs, rituals, tales of life back home.

This book has given the participants an opportunity to share their stories with others, but there are many isolated elders who still remain invisible. This work needs to continue and be developed, whether through future projects or through initiatives by community groups and their managers; otherwise it will be the black and ethnic minority elders themselves who will become just a distant memory.

Chapter One: Childhood Home & Family

CHINESE ELDERS

Mr Ke Wing Pang

I was born in 1935 in a village in the New Territories, an area of Hong Kong. My village was quite large, almost a town. My house was surrounded by farmland and lots of trees, but I could hear the trains as the railway line ran close by. I remember the weather was relatively warm, not usually hotter than 29 degrees.

Back then the old houses only had one bedroom and one sitting room. Mine was a one-floor house with an attic upstairs which was used for storage. The whole house had only two windows, one at the front and one at the back. I slept in the backroom, where there was one bed for my parents and one bed I shared with my siblings. There was an extra bed in the sitting room. We just had these two spaces, plus a little area where we could make our tea and boil soup. The house was open-plan but we had a divider to separate the bathroom from where we slept. For bathing we would have used a bucket and a small jug. At dinner time a folding table would have been put in the main room. We didn't have much furniture just some small wooden chairs. There was also a proper kitchen, which was used for lots of cooking, making dinners and boiling water for baths. Houses then didn't have running water, so we had to boil water, and firewood was used as fuel to heat everything up. In every house, there was an altar for prayers: you prayed to the god of the area and remembered all the people who had died in the area.

I was the youngest of three in my family, I had an elder brother and an elder sister. Altogether there were five people in my house. We were a family of farmers, my grandfather and his father were farmers. It wasn't just my family who were farmers; mostly all the families in my village were, but we could only afford to

FESTIVALS

Dragon Boat Festival

This involves a special boat race with beautifully decorated boats which are ten meters long. This festival commemorates the death of a popular Chinese national hero, Qu Yuan, who drowned himself in the Mi Lo river over 2,000 years ago when he protested against the corrupt rulers. The legend has it that the townspeople tried to rescue him by beating drums to scare the fish and they also threw dumplings in the sea to stop the fish from eating Qu Yuan's body.

Ghost Festival (August/September)

For one long lunar month during the ghost festival, ghosts are said to roam the earth. In this month Chinese people do their best to avoid late nights and steer clear of spirits. In some areas of Hong Kong small fires can be seen on roadsides and believers burn paper money. Other offerings such as new harvested grain are given to restless and departed spirits.

Moon Festival

Celebrated in the 8th month, it is a major holiday. It is an occasion for family reunions. Families get together and eat moon cakes which are like sweet biscuits with fillings. The round shape symbolises family reunion. Afterwards the family sits together and watches the moon.

rent the land. My father mainly grew rice and sweet potatoes. Everyone worked on the farm, men and women, it was a long, hard day! We would normally get up at six in the morning but if seedlings needed to be planted my family would get up around five. The crops were planted at certain times of the year. November was the time for growing sweet potato. We would harvest two crops of rice, one at the end of February and one at the end of May or beginning of June. My father kept some of the crops for us to eat and sold the rest.

It was a hard life, my family really struggled, they didn't have a lot of money, it could take up to three months from the day we planted the crop to the time we actually harvested. Then next month we could get the rice and sell it. After a long day's work in the field, my family would all sit together and have an evening meal of rice, vegetables and salt fish.

I really looked forward to the festivals because it gave me an opportunity to visit the city. I used to go with my friends and we would travel by bicycle. I didn't ride one myself, but I would sit on the back of my friend's bicycle. The Chinese calendar is very different to the British one and festivals took place at different times of the year. The fifth month of the Chinese year we would celebrate the Dragon Boat Festival. The seventh month we would celebrate the Ghost Festival. In the eighth month of the year we would celebrate the Moon Festival in my own village.

Mrs Phuong La

My birth home was in Macao, China. Back then, Macao was a Portuguese colony. I grew up near the coast. The town was full of mansions belonging to wealthy business people, as well as small houses and lots of gambling casinos. Macao was very green, we had seasonal weather like Hong Kong and it was not too cold. My favourite season was autumn because it was nice and cool.

In my childhood home, the lounge and the kitchen were both on the ground floor and the bedrooms were on the second. My father didn't like me and my sister going out, so he bought us a ping-pong table. I spent a lot of my time in the lounge, playing ping-pong and learning how to sew.

We were a family of four, I had an older sister who was four years older than me. My family raised me as a Buddhist, but through my schooling I took an interest in Catholicism. My father worked as the cook on a cruise ship, he would go in the mornings and come back in the evenings as the ship sailed to nearby places, often bringing gamblers to the Macao casinos and taking them back afterwards. He would have to buy the food before he reached work and cook the meals everyday. I remember he used to get up very early around six in the morning and he didn't get back until midnight or later. My mother was a housewife. She stayed at home and took care of us.

Mrs Ah Poh Luong

I was born in Vietnam around 1935. I grew up in a place called Poh Wan which is near the sea. I was actually born on a boat, so I am one of the sea people. My childhood days were spent on this houseboat. We also had a little rowing boat which my siblings and I used to paddle to the village market to buy food and to get water. We also used it for our own adventures.

The boat we lived on was small, there were no rooms. There was a covering built on top, like a house. Our parents slept towards the front and my sisters and I slept at the back. My brothers slept in the other boat.

My father was a fisherman. He had his own fishing boat which he used to catch

and sell fish. After a day's fishing, a larger boat would come and buy the fish from my father. They were fishermen just like my dad. Whatever my dad didn't sell was cooked for our meals. We mainly ate fish, rice and vegetables and very little meat, which was only eaten on special occasions. Like my father, other boatmen used to come and sell vegetables. They weren't very expensive.

We had to get used to all kinds of weather living on the boat, I remember there were really rough winds between June and August. When it got windy we had to drop little anchors and tie the boat up to stop it from drifting off. After an hour or so it would have calmed down.

As a child I remember every year in March we celebrated Cheng Meng Festival of the Dead. Everyone went to the cemetery and prayed to the dead. This was an occasion where we bought meat, it was given as an offering to the dead and then you ate it afterwards. It was one of the biggest celebrations and for that and Chinese New Year's Day, no-one went out fishing, everyone celebrated.

Mrs Mooi Tran

I was born in 1924. I grew up in Saigon, Vietnam. Saigon was generally a very hot city but from November onwards it starts getting cooler. I lived in a very busy part of the city, on the main street near to businesses and shops. It was such a built up area, it didn't have very many parks and

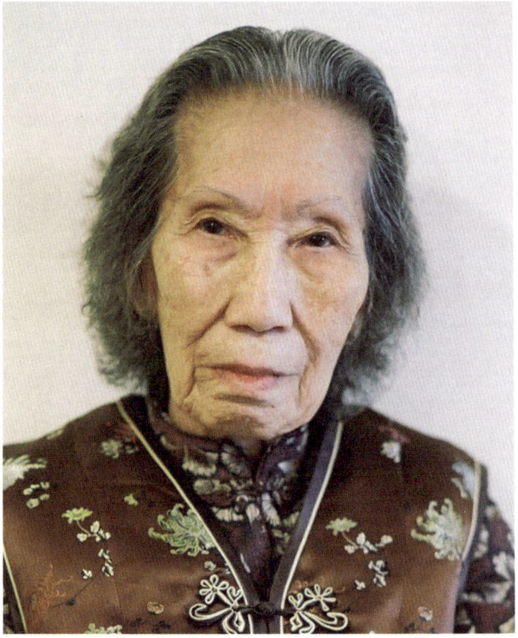

we didn't even have a garden. If I wanted to see flowers, trees or parks I would have to travel very far.

My childhood home was not very big. It had two floors, the two bedrooms were on the top floor of the house. There was one for parents and one for the children. I had one brother and one sister, I was the youngest in my family. Downstairs there was a lounge and the kitchen. At dinner we sat at a round table. I remember my mother cooking in clay pots on an open fire. The clay pots were placed on a brick frame with a hole in the middle for the firewood.

I am the youngest in my family, I have one elder sister and one elder brother, there are five in the family. I didn't call my brother and sister by their first names, I had to call my elder brother Tai Koi which is the standard Cantonese way of addressing your brother. Tai means big, Koi means brother and Chai is sister. My brother was ten years older than me and my sister was about six years older than me.

My father owned a Chinese medicine shop and he sold all types of herbs. My father and my older brother ran the shop and it was situated at the front of the house. At the back of the shop there was a door that led to the house, and, while my father and brother worked in the shop, my mum was busy doing housework and looking after us.

Mrs Makfung San

I am 83 years old. I was born in the city of Tong Tang in North Vietnam. There were many factories there; they made everything and there were farms around the city. My parent's business was selling rice.

They were wholesalers, buying everything, selling everything. When I was young there were a lot of French people in the city. My father and mother spoke French and were trading with the French.

Mrs Suk Tsang Tang

I am 72 years old. I was born in China, in Kut Yang, Canton in 1931. When I was eight, my family moved away, because at that time China was at war with Japan,

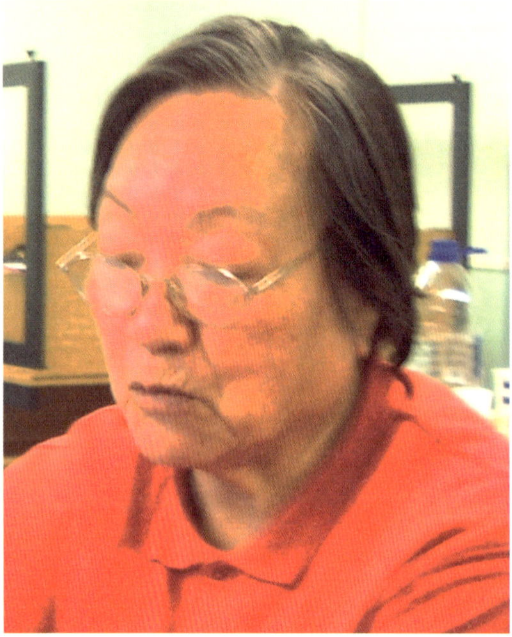

and they would have forced my father to be a soldier to fight the Japanese. But my father didn't want to be a soldier, so that's why he ran away, to escape. He took all the family, including me and my sister.

The day after my father escaped, the government stopped anyone from leaving the country. Then no one was allowed to run. So we were very lucky to get out in time. And Japan started bombing the place where we lived just after we left.

We went to Cambodia first, before going to Vietnam. My father's work was to carry the cargo from the ships. They had no machinery for lifting; they just carried things on their shoulders. Really heavy things like timber in the docks. From 1942 to 1952 we were in Cambodia. My father died in Cambodia, and in 1952 my mother and all the children went to Vietnam. My father's relatives were in Vietnam, and we looked for those relatives so they could help us to settle there.

AFRICAN ELDERS

Mrs Belmont Williams

I was born in 1931 in Freetown, which is the capital of Sierra Leone in West Africa. Sierra Leone lies on the coast bordering on the Atlantic Ocean. There are numerous rivers and lakes and many beautiful beaches with lovely white sands. Sierra Leone is blessed with a natural and scenic beauty. The climate is tropical, meaning that there are two well-defined seasons, a rainy season from May to October and a dry season from November to April. In addition, there is the harmattan, a very dry wind from the Sahara Desert which blows sand and dust from December to February.

My parents' home was in Clive Town on the outskirts of Freetown. The residential houses and buildings in the capital city and large towns are constructed from cement, sand, stones and corrugated iron sheets, but in the villages they are constructed with mud and wattle (sticks put together like a frame and the spaces filled with cement) and with bamboo and straw roofs. Sierra Leone used to be a peaceful and beautiful country. It is richly endowed with mineral resources such as gold,

bauxite, and diamonds. Fish is plentiful and the soil is fertile everywhere.

The nuclear family is rare in Sierra Leone. The main type is the extended family. My family consisted of my father, mother, one brother and three sisters, but there was always at least three other children growing up with us as brothers and sisters. My parents brought these children up as if they were their own. There was no discrimination between them and us. We shared the housework equally between us. When we were little, our mother did the cooking. But as we grew older we, the children, learned how to cook and we had much pleasure in doing so. By the age of twelve I was able to buy commodities from the market and cook food for the whole household. In my family, the girls as well as the boys learned to cook, do the washing up, laundry, ironing and cleaning of the home. We had a houseboy who did the heavier manual work.

My mother taught me to sew and to do every types of needlework and handwork including embroidery, knitting and crochet. Consequently, right from an early age I was making my own clothes as well as those of my sisters.

We took part in various celebrations in the home. These included the naming ceremony for the newborn, which involved placing a piece of the placenta or umbilical cord in a hole in the ground with a seed of a plant or fruit tree. The tree embodies the child and his or her connections to the universe. Following that, we usually celebrated the fifth, tenth and twenty-first birthdays. Weddings were celebrated, and the parents usually had their friends and other family members invited to a small gathering on their birthdays. I am a Christian, so I participated in the various festivals in the Christian calendar. Our family however had many Muslim friends and we shared food and gifts with them during our religious festivities and they reciprocated during theirs.

Mrs Josephine Macpeppele Ja Ja

I was born in 1938 in Anwu Hospital, Crossrivers State, Oron, Nigeria. My parents came from Opobo town. It's on the seaside. But when I was born they

were living in Oron and working in Calabar, a nearby city. We lived in a compound next to the riverbank.

We slept in a bungalow with one room for my parents to sleep, although my mother had her own room as well, and I had my own bedroom. The bath-house was separate and the kitchen was in another building because of all the smoke. We cooked with firewood. The stove we cooked on had three legs. The pot would have been placed on top with a fire underneath. I was very close to my parents, especially my father, Abraham. I loved being with them. My mother, Evelyn, wasn't working but my father was. He was a manager at the United African Company (UAC). My father dealt with the paper work; if there were any problems they called him. He dealt with the workers who would load palm kernels onto the ships docked near the sea, like you have in Liverpool. When the sun came out, they'd put them on a stretched sheet like a trampoline to dry them out, because some of them were not quite dry. Once they were dried, they would barrel them or put them in big bags, sew them and heap them up. My father's company also made palm oil products by extracting oil from palm kernels. The palm oil is an ingredient used to produce soap such as Palmolive. They transferred my father from Oron to Egwanga, now called Akwaibon state.

Mr Ade Aderogba

I was born in the year 1942. I grew up in Oshogbo in the South West of Nigeria. Oshogbo is a large town, the capital of Oshun State. The Nigerian climate is very tropical, the average rainfall is about 50 inches a year.

I am a Yoruba, which is one of the largest social groups in West Africa. My mother was a great Muslim leader. She died a couple of years ago when she was ninety. Her family actually brought Islam to the city.

I lived with my family in a traditional African family house compound. There were many rooms. The father's room was known, in colonial Africa, as the 'master bedroom' and the wives and the children had their own bedrooms. It was a very happy and typically African Yoruba environment.

My mother had six children and all six – touch wood – are alive and well today, which was very unusual given the mortality rate. Mine was a happy family. Something many people do not know is that women have a very prominent role to play in Islam, but not a political role. My mum wore the trousers in my family. She was a very powerful woman. She sorted out our education and each of my siblings got a good one. She was very keen on education. My mother was also a trader, selling clothes and so on.

My father worked for a French company known as CFAO. They were established in Nigeria in 1902 and he worked for them for thirty-five years, almost his entire working life. Because my dad was working for a French company, he would come home with French chocolates and French manufactured goods, and we called him Papa Français. To work for a foreign company in those days was an elitist situation and my contact with white people was established at a very young age. The CFAO in Nigeria was dealing with produce such as cocoa, cola nuts and palm kernels for shipping to France and my father was a clerk. I remember as a child, going to the CFAO compound in Oshogbo where they graded the cocoa into various categories. They weighed them, my father meticulously recording the different weights, and paid the farmers, and so on. That was my first impression.

My father also had a farm, every Nigerian of his generation used to have a small farm, so at weekends we were taken to the farm to help with the cultivation of cassava and yam. I could still tell you how to prepare cassava into garri, which is the most popular staple diet in West Africa.

My father had two wives. It was the norm. It would have been, perhaps, less than 10% of people of his generation that were monogamous. Monogamy wasn't a Yoruba thing. In fact, I remember asking him and he said he more or less had to, he was expected to take a second wife. Even today, I am sad to say, that polygamy is alive and well in Nigeria. And of course you have the Muslim influence and we were a Muslim family. Muslims can

The Shango
The Shango is the God of Thunder. Shango is one of the big Gods, you will see a Shango shrine in our compound in Oshogbo that is called Ilea Mogba. The Mogba is the chief priest of Shango. Shango is one of the original African religions and it is still one of the most important in Africa.

Oshun Festival
The Oshun festival is world-famous and is the worship of the river Oshun in Oshogbo. That is why the area is called Oshun State. There are thousands of visitors every year, even today, coming from America and different parts of the world to Oshogbo, to worship during the festival. The Oshun and Shango festivals are probably over a thousand years old.

theoretically take up to four wives. I have been monogamous myself. I have been married for thirty-six years. I don't believe in polygamy, but for my fathers' generation perhaps it was the right thing to do.

I felt I had two mothers. They were like sisters to each other. I have no recollection of any quarrel or fighting or noise. They were very peaceful. My mum was the senior wife, so she was accorded the role of being the mother of the family. She was about ten years older than the second wife, who just saw her as an auntie. As there were two mothers in the house and plenty of children, there were three or four domestic helpers from other tribes – another characteristic of Nigeria at that time. I am still against that, it is still persisting today all over West Africa, that so-called privileged tribes and privileged people will go into the village and bring young boys and girls for labour as domestic servants.

We used to have dual celebrations, Islamic festivals on the one hand, and the Shango and Oshun festivals on the other, celebrated especially by our grandparents. We were always celebrating something or the other.

Mr Anthony Maduagwu
I was born in the southern part of Nigeria now known as Imo State. I am an Ibo man. I was born in 1936 in a village called Nneogwugwu, where we lived in mud houses, but from the age of five I was brought up in Yaba, a crowded area of Lagos, which was then the capital of Nigeria. In Lagos it was bit more developed than some of the surrounding villages and life there cannot be compared with village life. As a child I remember living in a brick-built house with a corrugated-iron roof. The climate in Nigeria is generally hot almost all the year round, it only changes towards Christmas when it is usually a bit cold and windy.

Well, my family consisted mainly of three children and my mother, as my father passed away when I was young.

Before my father died, he worked in the civil service. So my mother brought all three of us up, but I can't say we struggled a lot because of the income from the shop my mother was running. She helped the whole family. I was raised as Catholic unlike other people in my community, who could marry and have as many wives as they could afford. To practice polygamy is not prohibited in my country.

We had a typical happy family life. Your parents woke you up early in the morning, saying, "You should have a bath and have your breakfast and go to school". In Nigeria the women do everything! Before I came here, I never stepped in a kitchen, to the extent that when I was coming to Britain my mum wasn't happy because she thought I would die of starvation. Well, now things are changing, but back then the male children were not allowed in the kitchen, only the female children. My mum did all the cooking. There was our staple food, ground rice. Back home, we used to have very palatable food and highly spiced. We'd have cassava, gari and yam. Mother also used to make soup with vegetables like okra, ogusi and agbolo.

As a family we celebrated Christmas. All the families who lived nearby cooked and offered food to one another. We also cooked and carried food to the other families. When Christmas came everyone was invited to sit down, have a meal, dance and play games. In the village you saw lots of people dancing with masks, it was like a carnival at Christmas time.

There were also traditional celebrations. Egwugu dancers performed masquerades during ceremonies at Christmas time and public holidays. The majority of the people who have gone abroad, or moved to the cities, go back to their villages to celebrate. Like when we have the Yam Festival, even here in this country, the Ibo people still celebrate it. When the time comes, they get together, have a party and raise funds. These celebrations are a kind of remembrance to the dead as well as a celebration of the living.

Mr James Adebayo Adesina

I was born in 1934 in Ibadan, Oyo state, Nigeria. Ibadan is a native city south of

the Sahara, originally founded as tribal war camp. By the time the missionaries and the British administration came, the tribal wars were stopped. Ibadan is in a savannah area, between grassland and forest. We have rainy and dry seasons so it is very good for agriculture. It is very fertile land.

My childhood home was made out of mud and the roofing was made out of iron sheeting. We didn't have any electricity but during that time it was considered a middle class African home. We had land around us, because we like space. Because of the tropical sunshine, you need a space under a palm tree where you can take cover in the daytime when it is very, very hot. The house was part of a big compound because all the family lived in the same place; the grandmother, the mother, the young girls, the second generation and the third: they would all live in that house. Everyone had their own room, but there was also a room where everyone could come and play, sit and socialise, all the extended family in one place.

Mrs Mako Herabe

I was born in 1933 in Warsheeq, Somalia, which is the nomadic area near the coast. My family were in the agricultural sector, we grew all the fruits, and made various breads. We had to bring these goods to the cities for people to buy and sell.

As I child, I grew up in a nomadic environment. In my culture the women are responsible for building the huts, the men gather and provide wood and other materials. I helped to build my family home with my sisters and my mother. We had a big hut large enough for a family of seven. A fence was built around the hut and it was surrounded by other huts. It was not like a typical house with rooms, everyone was living together, there were no separate rooms for the children.

When I was 16, I went to Mogadishu, the capital of Somalia, so I was able to be a link between the city and my home. Mogadishu is a tropical city with plenty of rain but also droughts. I built my first hut there out of wood and sealed together with cow dung. In Somalian it is called lamyerie. The roof is made out of very thin silver plate to cover and protect the inside.

My family consists of seven members, which includes two sisters and three brothers. I was in the middle – two boys were bigger than me and two girls were younger than me. My role was to look after the goats and the lambs. The men in the family had to take care of the cows but all the women looked after the goats. So my father and the boys had to look after the cows. This job involved collecting water and finding where the grass was for the cows to graze. Sometimes they had to walk at least three or four miles from where we lived. That was the man's job, the women had to remain behind and take care of the home. Water had to be fetched two days a week for the family.

As we lived near the coast in Warsheeq my father would trade with other businessmen. The livestock produced milk and this was made into ghee (purified butter) which was exchanged for money. We also traded with other people who had grain. So my father traded with other families. There were more than 2,000 people living in the area, because it consisted of three different working communities: livestock, agricultural (crops), coastal (fishing). People travelled to the main city and the markets to trade. Everybody brought what they had and they just bought and sold.

We were taught from a very young age to be responsible. So our parents instructed us until we were ten and then we had the responsibility of finding grass, fetching water, trading and looking after livestock.

Mrs Hawa Ismail Mumin

I was born in 1933 in Baargal, North Western Somalia. I was raised in a nomadic family. Somalia has a long coast, all around the North and Eastern side of the country. Boosaaso was the main city where nomads used to go and trade. My home was a traditional nomadic hut, a communal hut for all the family to share. The men and the older children slept outside to keep an eye on the livestock, and the women and the younger children slept in the hut. The weather was not very cold, we just had our clothes to sleep in. We didn't have any furniture like beds and chairs; the whole house was empty. We used to sleep on soft mats which we wove ourselves, or animal skins. I remember that when the weather turned bad we had to pack up our homes and move on. The goods and the hut were packed-up and it became a mobile home. We moved from one place to another to another. Camels were our transportation. Weather was not the only reason for moving as most nomadic families owned livestock and moved to where there was grass and water.

I grew up in Baargal with my two brothers, two sisters, mother and father. I was the middle child, but we also lived with our extended family. Everyone was very close, it is not only the mother and her children. Everybody looked after each other.

Our life was a nomadic one, where we were reliant on our livestock. We were only using our milk to drink and ghee to cook. We lived very far from the cities and had no-one close to trade with. Everyone in our tribe had the same thing, livestock! My father and brother had to travel along the coast to trade, until they reached the main city of Boosaaso. They used to work on the harbouring ships where they unloaded livestock, handicrafts and incense. They spent three or four months there until they could get some money and buy extra livestock for the family. That is how the family kept going.

Every morning we would wake up with the sunrise and pray. We would have something to drink and clean out the goat's pen. The adult women would be making ghee from the milk and preparing food and washing clothes with a plant called *gasangas*. This plant was used as soap to clean the clothes, we didn't have soap or washing powder like you do here. For example, when we used to wash utensils and dishes we would wash with sand or ash and water. We were surrounded by land and there was nothing to do except look after the animals and interact with friends and family. We were with the livestock from sunrise to sunset and they ate as much as they could in that time. We ourselves were not allowed to eat anything during that time. We couldn't even milk the animals, it was forbidden. However, we did not go hungry because there were lots of trees and we were allowed to eat their fruit and the seeds. We returned to the family and that is when we got our dinner. People were not the priority; animals were! We were raised to protect the livestock and we had to protect them from wild animals. We were never afraid, we used to see lions and foxes. If we saw a lion heading towards the livestock, about 10 to 20 children would just bang everything and shout very loudly. If animals did come, they used to take one or two livestock. In the nomadic area, no-one fears anything, but here I am even scared of cats!

Nomadic culture is about the open land, your job is to go and find water and grass for the livestock, and all you care about is the animals and nothing else. We sing a song for rain called *Come, Come* because we want the water so we can have grass and produce. The children also participated, singing songs about relying on the rain and the coming of the drought. We sang, "Come, come, come, I can smell the rain, so all the water will be around, the goats will be happy... the rain will be falling and everyone will be happy." If there is a heavy rainfall and a possibility of a flood, you have to take all the goats and put them on high land or a mountain. If the water goes straight to the animals they will be sick, so we shelter them in the caves.

Everyone had rice to eat because of the trading that took place. We had white rice with yoghurt. That is all we ate. At night we had more fun! All our traditional storytellers competed to compose the best songs that described something like, for example, a tree – its qualities and flaws. That was our literature.

The whole community came together to make music. There were big families and it was a very close-knit community. Even if the people didn't know anything about composing, they still sang, rehearsed and played instruments as well.

CARIBBEAN ELDERS

Mrs Irma Reid

I was born on 13th November 1944 in Cumana village, Toco, Trinidad. Cumana village wasn't developed. We didn't have

Cacao Plant
When you open the cacao plant you have a pod full of beans which look just like coffee beans. We would collect the beans and sell them. Some of the people in the village had cacao plants or bananas or whatever growing in their yard.

electricity and we had to go to a standpipe for water, which was like a normal tap by the road side. People had to go and fill carriers called pitch oil tins, bring them home, and put the water in drums. Usually this type of work was done by the grand-parents. Back then people who lived in the country didn't have proper wooden or concrete houses. People had to build houses with whatever materials they had; some were built out of a mixture of dung and white lime (a mixture known as Lepay) and the houses were referred to as 'dirt houses'. Those who owned estates would have given local people bits of land where they could build their houses. Other people in the village would have helped them. The roof would have been thatched. My grandparents' home didn't have cookers or stoves as such, but they made a 'fireside' from a mixture of mud and cow dung which was bound together and shaped it into an oval. It was painted with a mixture of white lime and water and my grandparents would have cooked on that with wood. The area where my grand-parents lived was full of different plantation estates of citrus fruits, cacao, coconuts and some spices. Women worked in the house but the men worked the cacao fields.

I grew up in San Fernando, it was very different to the village I was born in. San Fernando is one of the main towns in the Southern part of Trinidad. We had had an old wooden house but it did have electricity and running water. Back in those days we didn't have flush toilets. The WC or latrine and shower were situated in the back of the yard, it was nice and secure and the shower was all-enclosed with the roof over it. Our house was about three feet off the ground, so we had a nice gallery. There was a sitting room and a dining room, there were no doors but dividers between the rooms except the bedrooms which had doors. The kitchen was quite modern, it had a kerosene stove, I remember my mother used to do a lot of baking. However, as the family grew, we moved twice, from San Fernando to Brechen Castle and then to Couva, where we lived in a nice neighbourhood in Couva with rows of houses and a really wide street with people of different ethnic backgrounds.

There were eight of us in our family, Mum, Dad and the six of us children. I had two brothers and three sisters and I was the second oldest. The house we lived in had two big bedrooms. We used to share one with my mum and all of us used to sleep in the main big bedroom, which was

San Fernando
Trinidad was once a colony of Spain, just as it was of Britain and France. Christopher Columbus 'discovered' Trinidad. That is why most of Trinidad has a lot of Spanish links because the Spanish colonised it much longer than the British.

nice. We had a big four poster brass bed with a 'tester' going around the top, which was like a railing with frills hanging off it. It originally belonged to my mum, but when my youngest brother got married in 1979, he took it with him. My dad had a smaller bedroom in the back of the house.

My brother and I used to run down to the seaside, I was a real tomboy! My mum used to come looking for us, we knew she was coming, so we would run back home. She greeted us with a belt hidden behind her back. She never really used to beat us. We used to run around the house with her chasing us until she got fed up. My dad was very strict though, we were not allowed to go and play at friends' houses.

My father was a policeman so we were better off than most people, my mother didn't work. She stayed at home. So Dad was a very prominent, dominant figure in our home and mum's was a secondary role. My father's job meant that he was stationed all over the country and sometimes he wouldn't be home for three or four days. I remember sometimes Mum would take us on the bus and we would spend the day at the police station and come back in the evening. We were well known in all the different stations! My father used to get a good wage and of course he was paid in pounds, shillings and pence in those days.

Mr Michael Roper
I was born in the year 1930 and raised in Kingston, the capital city of Jamaica. It was a very busy place. I lived in a residential area called McQueen Street and I remember the tramcars that used to run along the avenue past my house. My childhood home was very similar to the place I live now. It was a very nice house located on the Eastern side of the city. I remember there being really nice houses along my

street. My house also had a veranda on the first floor.

I was an only child. I lived with my mother. My dad didn't live with us but he lived close by and we used to get on all right. He was a potter and he had his own pottery workshop which was down the street from us. I remember he had a nice big yard where he did his pottery. He made jars, all different kinds of jars. He used to make sewer pipes for the city corporation. He didn't work on his own. He employed other people to help make the pipes.

My mum was an ordinary worker, dusting the offices. She worked from seven to ten in the morning and then came and went back several times a day. The place she was working, the court library, her cousin was in charge. So he promoted her and she started working in the library. She would sort out all the law books in that place. It was really my cousin's job. But because she organised the library so well, he gave her more work. She knew exactly where books were, she was good at that.

What I remember most about where I lived were the tramcars. It was the main way of getting into town. When I was about ten, I used to get on the tram to visit my grandmother who lived in Constance Spring, twelve miles from Kingston, or she would come and visit us. There was a big park which we had to cross to drop her off at the tram station when she wanted to go home. She had a big walking stick and she said, "What a damn cheek to send me to a totally dark terminus", I had to move fast because she hit me with that stick, I am telling you! Then I saw her off on the tram.

Mrs Gladys Smith

I was born on the Caribbean island of St Vincent. We were four children, Mum and Dad, two boys and two girls so we were evenly balanced. I am number three and I think that's why they called me Gladys, because my mother was so glad: she had two boys before she had me

My father was a shoemaker, sometimes I passed by his workplace and helped him. I was the only one who was interested in his work and was always keen to help. It wasn't long before I was able to make three quarters of my own slippers. If he wanted

anything I'd know exactly what he wanted – I knew all his tools by name, he had an awl, pincers, stirrup, blakeys – I don't remember what they called the wheel they used. I don't think my brothers were interested in his work, but I was. He made really very lovely men's shoes. I don't remember him doing many ladies' shoes or doing many dress shoes, just everyday ones. He made all my shoes, I was the envy at my Girl Guides club. It was a joy to have shoes made by my father. Though, I can tell you, sometimes I would be in tears waiting for them. They were always put aside, you know, it was always, "Oh, you have another day or two to wait" or "I'll do it tomorrow." But I always had them in the end.

Mrs Hyacinth Thomas
I was born in Antigua, West Indies and was brought up by my grandmother. She lived in Antigua. They say Antigua has 365 beaches. I don't think I've seen a quarter of them. I think I've been to maybe five or six of those 365 beaches. My mother lived in Barbuda, so I have memories of two places. When I was at school I stayed with my grandmother in Antigua. There were chores that I had to do before I went to school: like fetching the water from the standpipe and sweeping the yard with the little coconut broom. In the afternoons I repeated the water part: I had to fetch more water because that's the water they used to do everything, the washing and the cooking. I had to do it twice a day. In Barbuda it was different. We didn't have a standpipe in Barbuda. You got the water from the wells. So you used to have to go to the well with a bucket tied to the end of the rope and draw the water from the well. I spent the school holidays with my mother in Barbuda. Barbuda was less developed than Antigua. For a long time there was no electric light.

In Barbuda I used to go to the seaside to pick up seaside grapes, which grow along the sea front. And there were coco plums. You could get loads of sugar apple in Barbuda, in the bushes. We ate mainly fish and venison, because the reindeers were wild. My stepfather used to go hunting in the evenings and fetch the reindeer, so venison for us was an everyday meal. Here it's a delicacy. We also ate wild pig, and land turtle.

To cook a land turtle you'd have to turn it on its back, chop both sides of the shell, then with your knife you take the belly shell off then you cut out the rest of it. What was funny about that was it never died until some time later because you had to take off the skin in hot water, so even when it's cut out of the shell, it actually dies when you put it in the hot water to take off the skin! It did taste good. You cook turtle like any meat. You brown it, and sauté in onions. You cook it like a beef stew.

During one of those holiday periods, my mother gave me two shillings to go and get some fish. I took the two shillings. Off I went to fetch the fish. But as I got to where the boats come in with the fish I could see the children swimming out to the boats because if you can get to the boat you have more choice of the fish. Sometimes by the time the fisherman comes to the shore all the fish is gone. So I thought, "How am I going to get this fish?" I thought, "I can't swim, but I'm not going to let anybody know that I can't swim." The reason for that is, when you come from Antigua and go to Barbuda, all the boys and everybody they're after you, they think that you are something special! So I couldn't let my side down. So I put the two shillings into a hanky, tied it on my waist and off I went pretending that I could swim. My feet never left the seabed but my arms were going the motion as if I was swimming. As I got to the boat, I lifted my hand, there was no hanky, no money! During the swimming motion, the hanky got loose and came off my hand. I started to cry because what am I going to go home to say? The money's gone, what am I going to do? Anyway the fisherman was sorry for me, so he gave me the fish. I took the fish home but I never said to my mother that this thing happened. I kept it as a secret.

There was always a celebration in the early days – they used to call it Jambull. That's where the word 'jamboree' comes from. A man would dress himself in straw skirts, his face masked, with two horns tied onto his head. So as a child we would go out to watch the festivities that were going on. Children used to be afraid that he would come after you. Children used to be afraid of this Jambull because he would be dancing with his skirt going and his horns. So by the time he gets close to you you're ready to run.

ASIAN ELDERS

Mrs Avtar Bilkhu

I was born in 1942 in a village called Bhullari in the Punjab. The main city was three miles away from my village. My village was a very beautiful place. It was a real community, but some people were

very poor as well. They had no shoes, no clothes, and there was little food.

It slowly, slowly improved in contrast to other poorer villages. As a young girl, I lived in a big brick house with my parents, brother and uncle. My father was an electrician so our house was the first house to have electricity. There was a main factory in the village which produced clothes. The factory is still there now.

I was the youngest in my family. I have got two sisters and one brother. However, I didn't grow up with my sisters they were both married by the time I was two years old. One sister lived in Ludhiana in Punjab and the other sister lived in Nairobi. I hardly saw them. By the time I was ten, my brother was married, but I went to his wedding. The only people I grew up with were my brother, mother, father and my uncle who never got married.

As a child I enjoyed playing games. My friends and I used to play at the back of the house which had a big field. We used to play badminton and even tried to play kabadi, a chasing game like tag. People think it is a game just for men, but women play it as well. We also played a traditional stone game called Pitu, like Five Stones or Jacks. I also enjoyed drawing and doing crafts like embroidery, crochet and knitting. My mother taught me everything.

My father had his own shop in a city called Phagwara, but he also carried out electrical jobs in the village. Through my dad, I learned how to do wiring. My father also fitted the pipes that went underneath the houses. My mum didn't work, she was a housewife. She was a very intelligent lady and an expert in cooking. My uncle did a lot for the community, and was very well-known. So that is my family, we were very happy.

Mr Fazal Rahim Shah

I was born in Pakistan in 1937, in the very famous and very ancient city of Multan, which is in the east. It used to be a state, in mogul times, but now it is a district. In Multan, the architecture is fabulous, the colour schemes and the representations of flowers. In Islam we don't paint pictures, but the graphic art is second to none. Even today, everywhere you go in Pakistan that

Multan artwork is repeated over and over again and you see the architectural style everywhere. The Moguls brought high culture with them and the city is also renowned for its Sufi saints who are buried there, and its literature. It's a very big town and is known in Pakistan for mango growing. Ninety-nine percent of the mango groves are in that area. It's very hot and very fertile and absolutely fabulous, every kind of green grows there such as wheat, rice, vegetables – you name it!

As a child I moved around from district to district with my family because my father was a high-ranking police officer, so wherever we moved, the house was already there. Somebody else moved out and we would move in. It was a swap – if an inspector goes into one town, the other inspector moves out. Because we didn't have a base of our own, my father kept us with him. Wherever he moved, we went, taking everything with us – animals, birds, furniture… everything moved! We were about twenty-one people moving around, including our servants. We had several trucks to help us move. We didn't do much – our people did the job of moving things around. We had basic furniture. We had animals – cows, buffalos, horses, because in those days every police officer must have a horse to go around on.

Looking back, I feel all the moving around wasn't so bad because I picked up every kind of dialect of the different areas of Pakistan. I experienced different communities, different cultures and a different way of living. I feel this enhanced my happiness, my life and gave me a very broad horizon.

There were ten in the family. We were four brothers and six sisters. Originally there were six brothers and six sisters, but two of my brothers died at a very young age. I am the middle child.

Being raised in a large family meant my father had to be a very tough man. But at the same time, he was a friend. Although my four brothers were older than me, I always called them by their names, so we were more like friends than brothers. We always went out as a group. If we wanted to go to the pictures, my father said, "Okay, I'll take you to the pictures". So we didn't stray, all four brothers stayed together all the time. We never argued, but if I got angry with my brother, instead of arguing with me, he used to walk away. Even now we remain very close.

I also had a very good relationship with my sisters. My oldest sister who has now passed away, brought us up. My mother had too much to do, so my sister stopped her studies and stayed at home. Back then in our country, women were not allowed to work, they got married! So she brought us up, especially me, being the youngest. She used to do all my chores – ironing, breakfast, everything. I don't remember my mother doing anything for me.

My father was an extremely influential person in my life; he was always jolly and full of fun. As my father was a high-ranking police officer he was well known wherever he went, because he was a very honest, hard-working and well-balanced man.

Mrs Pramila Desai

I was born in 1936 in Sojitra in the district of Kharad, Gujarat, India. At that time the town was filled with village people who would have go to the well and fetch water. The water came from the pipe but you couldn't drink it because it tasted sour. Rich people paid the poor to fetch drinking water, but the village water was used to wash clothes.

In my town some local people had land and mainly worked as farmers, but some also had businesses. My father was a

businessman, so he could afford to build a brick house. It was a very good house, two storeys high and at the top of the house we had a flat rooftop, so you had all these places where people could sleep, because India is very hot in summertime. Our house was surrounded by lots of land outside. When you entered my childhood home you came into the sitting room. I remember people used to sit on the floor, because it was so hot and the floor was nice and cool. My mother and I slept on the first floor and my father and brothers slept on the second.

My father had 75 mango trees, we would keep some for ourselves but he would sometimes give them to the poor people. I remember how my mother used to make chutney with the small mangoes. There were always jars filled with sweet pickle. People would come into my father's shop and he would just give them the jars of mango pickle because there was always too much! My childhood home is still there now and I have visited it a few times since I came to England, such as when my son got married.

My father ran a textiles business. He got up around 9.00 am to open the shop. He sold all types of materials for saris. He used to order materials to sell from Madras, because people couldn't go there as it was too far from our town. The shop was near my house, it was a five minute walk. Only my father worked in the shop apart from one servant. He would come home at lunchtime then he would go back to work. My mother didn't work; she took care of the house, she was always cooking plenty of food, we always had people coming for food. I remember the door always being open in our house, not like here. People were always coming in. Everyone was really friendly to each other.

I had two brothers and three sisters. I was the youngest in my family. My oldest brother was a very good friend of Mahatma Ghandi. When Ghandiji was in jail and we were fighting the British for freedom he was also in jail with Ghandiji. He always wore hand-loomed garments like Ghandiji even though my father had a clothes shop. He campaigned with Ghandiji and I met him when I was ten years old as he came to my house. Ghandiji and my brother were giving a lecture in the town on the British and freedom, I put a flower harl (garland) on him. Back then I didn't completely understand who Ghandiji was, but I learned a little about him at school, that he was fighting for our country. My brother got an award from Indira Ghandi.

Mr Bagwant Singh

I was born 1931 in the city of Dar es Salaam, Tanzania, East Africa. I remember there was a port but our family moved around a lot when I was very young so I don't remember much about my birthplace. We moved around a lot because of my father's job; he worked for the railways. My family were from India and I think they migrated in 1924. They migrated for the usual reasons, for better prospects and because it was an all-British colony and India was under British rule. In the olden days, my father travelled from India by ship to Africa. So my childhood was spent mainly in Tanzania, then known as Tanganyika.

I lived in many parts of East Africa because my father used to be transferred every three or four years from one place to another, to towns or cities or stations according to his job. We travelled the whole of East Africa, so I didn't really have one home. We moved to places such as Dar Es Salaam, Moshi, Kondoa, Tegoma. The railways provided the accommodation.

One of the places I remember fondly was Moshi, near Mount Kilimanjaro. The

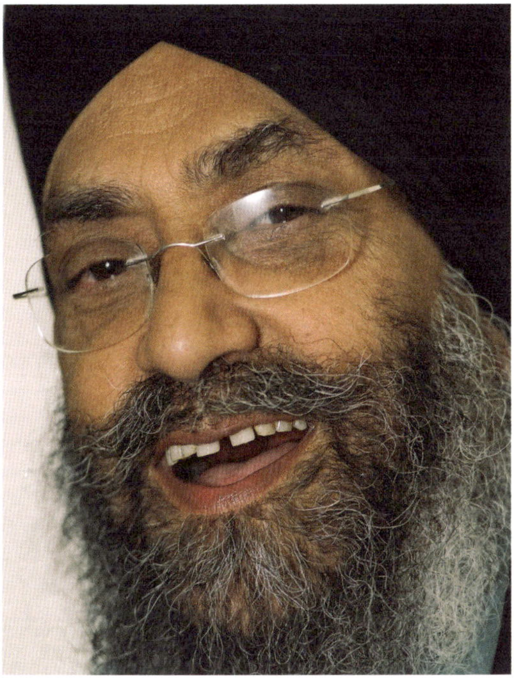

house I lived in was originally used as a kind of hospital during the Second World War. It was a small hospital, made of brick and mortar and almost square with a kitchen and couple of big rooms, a bathroom and toilet. In Africa all the houses have a slanting roof made of steel corrugated sheets. This house was very neat and we kept it very nicely. The railway line ran from Moshi to Arusha. The place where I grew up was very nice and very calm. We were surrounded by jungles and sometimes you could see lions and hyenas. There was no electricity, and rations were provided by the railway. I went there last year, after 15 years, just to see that place! We had a look inside and we stayed there maybe an hour and saw my father's office – it was wonderful to remember again!

My father was a Permanent Railway Inspector (PRI). He was responsible for five hundred miles of track, he had to inspect it every two or three weeks and he used one of those trolleys called a bogey. There were four workers who took turns to check everything was okay. I remember they used to tell funny stories about a rhino lying on the tracks! Behind the railway house was a chumba which is a garden. My father used to grow all kinds of vegetables, we even had a small reservoir but the water has gone now. It has all been destroyed and they have built a house over it, which is a bit sad.

While my father was working my mother was taking care of us. Although she was isolated from other neighbours she wasn't lonely, she had us five sons and three daughters to keep her occupied and she had the servants to keep her company. It was a good life over there, it was very nice.

A typical day would have been getting up and sitting in the kitchen with my brothers and sisters. Mum would be cooking parathas (Indian pancakes) then she would get us ready for school. After school I would come home, have tea, mostly in the evenings we just played around. We went to bed early because we did not like sitting around when it got dark. We had small paraffin lights that we used to put on and go to bed.

Mrs Sheila Rakhit

I was born in 1942 in Bengal. My family were not rich, but we were comfortable, so I was fortunate. Our house was built on top of a hill and it had a tinned roof. When the wind blew, the branches of the mango tree next to the house rattled in a rhythm on the tinned roof. During the monsoon season, I could hear on some nights the howling of the wind when it hit the tin roof. In the morning, I would go outside to find lots of mangoes scattered all over the back yard and I picked up those ripe mangoes in my folded skirt. Coming inside, I made mango pickled chutney and finished by licking my fingers. I can remember exactly the taste of it to this day.

Our house had a long open verandah where I used to sit on a cane chair. Sitting there in the morning sun, I gazed at the palm tree where I could see the hanging nests of weaver birds and hear the chirping of the birds. Some of the mother birds were still busy making their nests flying backwards and forwards bringing straws in their beaks one at a time, gathering into incredible shapes. Some looked like a vase or a jug. That was an amazing sight watching them at work.

I also remember vividly how we used to celebrate Diwali, the Hindu festival of lights. It is also a festival of sharing love and happiness with others. At that time, we used to decorate the house with flowers, and the perfume used to fill the whole house. At the front of the house, near the main entrance door we put rangoli, a special painting made from rice flour paste, on the floor as a welcoming sign. We also used to light earthenware lamps with three wicks which surrounded the whole front of the house. The house looked enchanting with dazzling lights. The adults used to blow a conch shell in a fine tune which used to fill my heart. This is supposed to be an auspicious ritual welcoming call for good luck, rather like a church bell ringing on a Sunday morning.

Childhood Home Creative Activities

OLDER PEOPLE'S ACTIVITIES

Introductions, or What's In a Name?

A good starting point is a name exercise in which people work in pairs, talking about their own name. Who gave it to them? Does it have a meaning? Is it a family name going back generations? Do they like their names? Have they changed their names?

The pairs can then report back some of their findings to the larger group, by introducing their partner and seeing how much they can remember of what was said. This exercise is a good way of emphasising the value of listening to everyone in the group and taking some responsibility for remembering what was said. Each partner should check if there is anything in what they have said in their pairs which they do not wish to share in the larger group. This reinforces the idea of mutual respect for confidentiality between story tellers and within the group. This is a very powerful exercise in learning about the backgrounds of different group members. However, one must be aware that one or two people may not want to talk about their names and may find the approach too personal, so group leaders must be sensitive to individual needs and not force the exercise.

A Basket of Memories

Pass round an empty basket and ask each member of the group to share what memories it triggers of their country of origin. What remembered object would they put into the basket from 'home' and what associated feelings and images are conjured up by it? The basket is a good icebreaker because everyone takes a turn, contributing as much or as little as they wish and it is a simple way of bringing together cultures and generations. The basket itself should be handmade, if possible, and well worn.

Three Words

Ask the group members to mention three words which come to mind when they think of the place where they grew up. These could be words describing a place, a sound, a smell, an action, a person or people, a photo taken there or a favourite food. Then ask people to work in pairs, sharing the memories which lay behind the words they first thought of. Some of these shared conversations can be relayed to the whole group, as this will probably help to trigger more memories.

Drawing a Memory

The previous exercise leads naturally into a drawing session, where group members can help one another to record what food was made, where it was cooked and served and who was there to eat it. This is a great opportunity to remember small details,

The Deptford Indo-Chinese group drawing their memories

which sometimes get forgotten when recording verbally. The drawings can be very diagrammatic with 'stick people' representing the different characters remembered. The purpose of the exercise is not to produce fine art, but to stimulate detailed recall and have a means of sharing it with the group. If the group work in pairs on this exercise, they can stimulate each other with questions and then jointly present their 'findings' to the rest of the group.

The World Beneath Your Feet

Ask the group to imagine that the floor is a map of the world. Agree which direction is north, south, east and west. Agree where you are now. Ask group members to go and stand on the part of the floor which can represent where they grew up. With eyes closed, they can visualise better their childhood home. Ask each person to say out loud two words which have come to mind during this exercise. Then ask people to share what first came to their minds with one other person. The same exercise can be done sitting in a group, but the choosing of a place on the map can stimulate warm exchanges, as people find themselves standing near to someone from the same region.

A Guided Tour

The people we have interviewed have remembered a great deal about the layout of their childhood home. Ask members of the group to take you on a guided tour of the place where they grew up, opening doors, seeing familiar pieces of furniture, noticing views from the windows and remembering where they slept or where food was prepared. This can be done in pairs or as a small group of explorers with a guide.

The above exercise can be extended to include the local area, including their school, the local shops, the nearest play space. Again the 'guided tour' approach, with the person remembering as the 'expert guide', will help to reinforce the confidence of the story-teller, the need for the group to listen to one another's particular experiences, and the pleasure of sharing memories held in common.

A Soundscape

Ask each member of the group in turn to think about the sounds around his or her childhood home. Examples might be the wind, birds, trains, ships' hooters, sheep, cows, market traders. Then the rest of the group can make a soundscape, each making a different noise.

On This Plate...

Another useful ice-breaker is to pass round a simple plate or bowl and ask members of the group to tell what they would put on it as a memory of food their parents or grandparents cooked for them. They may remember smells and tastes, likes and dislikes. Often people will spontaneously remember the circumstances under which food was prepared and eaten.

Cooking Up Memories

Many storytellers remember favourite foods, often made from local produce. Collect together some of the favourite recipes of people in the group into a small booklet. It is fun to try to re-make some of these if cooking facilities are available, using the methods the older people remember their mothers using as far as possible. If you are able to photograph the group preparing the food and the finished dishes, these images could be illustrations for the booklet. Eating the results together is a good way to celebrate all that has been remembered.

Everything Fresh

Fresh fruit and vegetables can act as an effective trigger for memories of childhood homes, since so many of the storytellers remember yards, gardens and open spaces where exotic fruits were always freely available. Bring in examples of the fruits and vegetables mentioned by the group and pass them round. As people handle and smell these, ask for their local name and a recipe using them, so that the group can make comparisons. If fresh food is not available to stimulate memories, it is a good start to show pictures of the main items remembered.

In My Family

Family organisation varies greatly according to culture. Which examples resonate most with the members of the group? Some examples from this chapter are: the extended family where everyone lives and eats together, the family with two mothers, the single parent family, the family where the father worked away from home, the family where the father was there but rarely seen because of long working hours, the nomadic family where generations work together taking care of livestock and building temporary huts.

Indoor Child or Outdoor Child?

Story-tellers remember very different kinds of childhood, from the child kept mainly indoors by protective and strict parents to the free-roaming child growing up outdoors and near to nature. What do group members think of as the space where they spent most of their childhood days? Can they draw, or ask you to draw for them, this space with themselves in it. The pictures can be quite diagrammatic (even 'stick-people') as the pictures are a means of retrieving memories, rather than a means of generating art works. If the result is attractive as well, this is of course a bonus, and these images can be displayed so that others become interested in what the group is doing.

My Family Tree

Some of the story-tellers have very large families with many siblings. Some may wish to try to represent their family tree, showing where all their brothers and sisters spent their lives and where they still have family members scattered across the world.

Arms Around the World

Putting some of these family trees together and comparing them is a fascinating way of seeing how worldwide are the contacts older people have and finding common links within the group.

YOUNG PEOPLE'S ACTIVITIES

Maps & Journeys

The story-tellers come from all over the world. Use maps from the internet or an atlas to see where their birthplaces are. Have some of the students got connections with these places? Can they draw a map to show how many parts of the world have family connections for them and show where members of their families have travelled to and from in the past?

When I Was a Child...

This chapter and the one which follows tell about childhood experience. Invite grandparents or great-grandparents of the students into the classroom to share their memories of their early days and to compare notes with today's children.

A Day in the Life...

Some of the storytellers grew up in the confined space of a boat and others in the wide open space of the desert, moving from one resting place to another, or within an extended family compound. Working in twos or threes, the students should select an environment which is very different from their own. They should imagine a day spent there as a child and write a diary entry for that day. The students might wish to look in the next chapter (*Growing Up*) to see how the person they have chosen develops their story, and use this information to help them with the task. Accounts could then be compared with others who have chosen very different environments.

Chapter Two: Schooldays & Growing Up

CHINESE ELDERS

Mr Ke Wing Pang

I started at school at the age of eight or nine. It was a Chinese school and I was mainly taught in Cantonese, but we had one English lesson a week. I left home at nine o'clock, and I didn't even have any breakfast. Both my parents were up early and working in the fields. I didn't eat until the evening and I went to school very hungry. Sometimes I would take in boiled rice and eat that! My parents would take their food and eat it in the fields. I would get home from school around 4.30pm and join my parents in the fields.

Only my brothers and I went to school. My sister helped my parents in the fields. Back then girls did not go to school, unless the families were very rich. I also had to attend school on Saturdays, which was a half-day. I finished school when I was 19 because I didn't really do that well. I stayed back quite a bit because you only went up a class if you did well.

My family had high hopes for me, but unfortunately there so much work in the fields they needed my help. Study didn't come first; work came first! As I got older I found it very difficult to find work. I wasn't trained in anything and I ended up doing manual work. I used to cut grass along the roads. I was paid $2.50 and the foreman kept 50 cents of my wage.

But it wasn't all hard work and we did have some fun, even though we didn't have a lot of money. I used to love going to the cinema. It was an open-air cinema which didn't have a licence. There was no roof and it was a fairly spacious building with numbered seating. There was a cover over the projector just in case it rained. If it rained for more than half an hour, the show was abandoned. However, the ticket could be used again for the next show. You couldn't go on your own; you had to be accompanied by an adult. Sometimes I didn't even have to pay. I could go in with someone who had a ticket. I used to really like going to the cinema, but I couldn't always afford it.

Mrs Phuong La

I went to a Catholic missionary school in Macao. It wasn't easy to get to, a really roundabout route from my house on the road, but there was a quicker way to go, climbing lots of stairs, so that is what I did. I was taught maths, writing letters, poems, literature, geography, classic Chinese and Portuguese, because of course Macao was a Portuguese colony at that point. We didn't use biros in our school, we were taught to use Chinese brushes and ink.

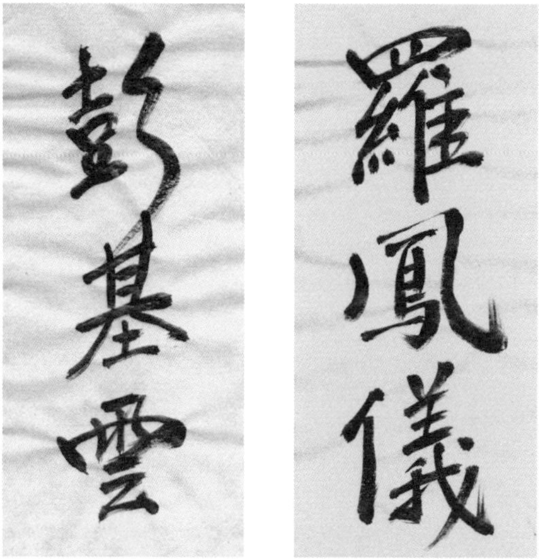

Chinese calligraphy showing Mr Pang's and Mrs La's names respectively

This was considered a respectable way to write. When writing to elders, we had a fixed way of addressing them but with my friends I used the colloquial way of writing. I learned Chinese and Portuguese writing but I have forgotten my Portuguese now.

I used to get up at 8am for breakfast and my mother used to make oatmeal and toast. I returned home at 4.30. My parents were strict. I had to do my homework straight away after school. I didn't like studying, I liked going to the cinema. I used to watch westerns and I really liked comedies. My father felt I spent too much time at the cinema and he decided to send me to boarding school when I was 12. The boarding school was part of my old school. I used to come home at the weekends. It was an all girls' school and it was run by Portuguese nuns. Some of the teachers were from my home town.

My mother really wanted me to be a midwife but, sadly, I lost both my parents when I was young and I couldn't study anymore after that. My father passed away when I was 13 and still at boarding school. My mother died two years later when I was 15. My sister got married at 20 and she and my brother-in-law had to support me. We moved to Hong Kong shortly after the funeral as my sister's husband had a business there.

The funeral was a difficult time as it was customary for the son of the family to carry out the funeral rites. As I didn't have any brothers, and my uncle had also died, the responsibility fell to his sons, my cousins. They did not want to carry out the full funeral rites because we didn't have any money or property to contribute, so nothing happened. There was no ritual and my parents were just buried. Normally, when a Chinese person dies you have a tablet which represents them and which is placed in the home. We had one for our father, but when my mother died, this did not happen. My sister was very angry with my cousins and, when one of them offered me a teaching job at his school, my sister refused to let me accept. Eventually, both parents' tablets were placed in the temple so someone could pray to them.

I spent my teenage years fleeing different countries because of the war. I was 15 when we travelled by boat to Hong

Kong. I lived there with my sister and her husband. We slept at the back of the shop. He used to buy hides and, depending on what kind of leather it was, he treated it. He did this by nailing it to a wooden frame. I used to help in the shop. It was a busy place. Unlike Macao which had 24 hour gambling, this wasn't allowed in Hong Kong because it was a British Protectorate.

After work I used go to the cinema with fellow workers. Sometimes we used to go swimming, I learned how to swim with my friends at the beach. I had more freedom and I even went to dance halls, where I learned to dance the quick-step and the waltz. My girlfriends and I used to get dressed up, but we didn't dance with the boys, we only danced with each other. I wasn't allowed to go out with boys. If I did, I would have had to get married. My sister was very strict about this.

I spent four years in Hong Kong, but we fled after hearing the Japanese were going to invade. We used to hear the sirens and there were many blackouts. We left at the end of 1940 and the Japanese came in 1941. We were so scared that we left Hong Kong. We went back to my birthplace, Macao, except for my sister's husband who remained behind to close the business down. He joined us shortly after that.

Mrs Ah Poh Luong

All my family lived on the boat. In total I had five sisters and three brothers. I was the youngest in my family. Most of my siblings stayed on the boat but two of my brothers used to go out fishing with my father. My younger brother stayed at home and studied, but I didn't go to school or study at home, because in those days boys were encouraged more than girls. I was one of the ones who couldn't read.

A typical day on the boat would have started with helping my mother with the chores like cleaning and helping my other siblings. I also did the sewing and made my own clothes. Other chores involved taking out the small paddling boat to collect firewood. We didn't have lights on the boat but kerosene lanterns, and wood was used to light the stove. While I was helping my mother, my father went fishing.

Mrs Mooi Tran

All three of us went to school in Saigon, Vietnam. In my time, 80 years ago, very few people sent their daughters to school, unless they were rich. My father had to pay fees for me to attend school. Some schools charged higher fees than others. I started at school when I was seven. I didn't go to the same school as my brother and sister; they went to a senior school, I went to a mixed primary school. I would get up at 8am and for breakfast I used to have conji. This was a plain broth, consisting of rice boiled until very soft and watery. We all had breakfast together, and afterwards my father would start work in the Chinese medicine shop. I went and got ready for school; my uniform was a white blouse and black skirt.

I used to walk to school everyday. On the way to school, the Vietnamese coffee shops would always be busy; they used to open at 4am. I used to see people carrying baskets of vegetables and fruit that they had purchased from the market. Before the lessons started, we would assemble in the playground. The bell would ring and we would go into our classrooms. Each year had their own classrooms, and I was taught by two teachers. I learned how to use the Chinese abacus. I looked forward to break time. We played games like ping-pong and netball.

School stopped at 11am for lunch. I went home for lunch, mother cooked rice with different vegetables. I returned to school by 1pm and finished at 5pm. After school, I returned home and I wasn't allowed to go out after that. I had to have a bath and do my homework. Even at the weekends I had to stay at home. This rule also applied to my sister and my brother. My parents were afraid that we would mix with the wrong type of people. In the past, girls were not allowed to go out. If your neighbours found out, then nobody would want to marry you because you would have a reputation! When I did go out, it was always with my parents.

My father didn't encourage me to come into the shop, especially when he was doing business. But I did go in when it was quiet and nobody was there. I would sit and talk to my dad and I liked to watch him at work. My brother was the only one who learned about Chinese medicine. Our duties focused on what we needed to know for marriage, celebrations and rituals.

My favourite celebration was Chinese New Year; I looked forward to receiving the presents in red packets and I always got new clothes. My mum bought these for me; I didn't get asked what I wanted.

Mrs Makfung San

I didn't need to do anything to help at home, because the family was quite rich from the wholesale business. So I didn't need to do anything. But they would only let the boy go to school. The girl wasn't allowed to go to school. So I didn't learn reading or writing.

AFRICAN ELDERS

Mrs Belmont Williams

I was initially educated at home and taught by my parents. My father was a teacher and very involved in education. I gained my secondary school education at the Annie Walsh Memorial School. Annie Walsh's parents were missionaries in Sierra Leone and the school was founded in 1849 by the Church Missionary Society with the

intention of grooming girls to become wives of the boys from the Church Missionary Society Grammar School, founded four years earlier. In school I took part in various sports like athletics and netball. I went on outings, sometimes with school groups, sometimes with my family or with friends. I went to the cinema, shows and plays. I had several friends and we visited each other. It was great being a teenager in Sierra Leone.

The need for more doctors in my country was brought home to me when I lived with my parents in the Protectorate. I had a deep desire to qualify and enter the medical profession. I can vividly recall the evening my parents asked me what I wanted to do when I finished secondary school. I said "Medicine". After a pause my mother said, "We cannot afford it". The problem was that I was the eldest of their five children. But my mother continued and said, "If you are to do Medicine, the Lord will provide." Well, the Lord indeed provided. At that time, science was taught in only one boy's secondary school, but I was lucky because I was one of the first five students to be enrolled into Fourah Bay College. This college was the first Institution of Higher Learning in West Africa and was affiliated to the University of Durham in England. We studied Physics, Chemistry, Biology and Mathematics. A few years later, I was awarded a full Scholarship by the British Government to study medicine in the United Kingdom.

Mrs Josephine Macpeppele Ja Ja

If we didn't go to church, our daddy would beat us. You had to go to church! When I returned home my father would ask me what the priest had said. My daddy was a churchwarden, so he knew if you were lying and whether you had gone to church. Some children were not in the church; they were playing outside. When I was older I joined the choir. My mother was also a good singer, and I sang a little. My favourite hymn was "Lord, I come unto thee empty handed. Nothing in my hand I bring. When I come I didn't bring anything, when I go I don't take anything."

I went to St George's School. The maids used to take me to school. I don't remember at what age I started school; we didn't know our age. The elders would ask us to put our right hand over our head to see if we could touch our left ear and if we could, we were ready for school. I enjoyed playing, but when it rained we used to hide under my daddy's porch. When I passed the Standard Three, they transferred me to the Methodist Missionary School. At that time I wasn't living with my parents. I had to live with the headmaster, because the school was too far and we didn't have a car or even a bicycle. The headmaster lived in the compound of the school. My uniform was a white shirt and blue skirt. We had European teachers; I remember one teacher was called Reverend Pete. It was a mixed school, so everybody played together. We used to celebrate Empire Day on 24th May. The boys took part in the sack race. I was in the bottle race, three-legged race, and the egg and spoon race. Prizes were awarded after the races. I never won any races, I always used to fall when I ran! The whole day was a big event with lots of food, and fundraising.

Mr Ade Aderogba
I went to a local primary school in Oshogbo. Then in 1957, I went to the College of Technology in Lagos. I really enjoyed school and I was always a keen student. My mother was a fantastic woman of her generation, for her it was education, education, education! That is why all six of us today are graduate-level professionals holding down good jobs.

In Nigeria and most of the colonies, the British had set up boarding schools that mirrored Eton and Harrow. These special public schools produced the 'crème de la crème of people' who took over after independence. Four thousand candidates from all around the country and from Cameroon (which was part of Nigeria at that time) applied for the sixty places at Yaba Tech Institute. I was one of those sixty. Whilst at Yaba Tech, I was never taught by a single black person. You woke up at 6am, had a cold shower and went out and played cricket or hockey. All the teachers were known as Federal

ADMINISTRATION BLOCK, TECH. INSTITUTE, YABA

Education Officers. They were selected through the Department of Education in England, but sent to Nigeria. So my education was incredibly public school based. I later sent my own three children to an English boarding school. They used to say, "Dad, you know how it feels – cold showers and boarding school troubles!"

The education that we had at Yaba was very special. We took the London University GCE exams. We were taught eight subjects, and were expected to get straight 'A's. The class on British History was very thorough, I could recite all the battles, the Norman Invasion and the Wars of the Roses. I always had 'A star plus' in English history! They didn't teach us African history, but I learned that from my family.

Growing up, I was always curious about what white people did. There was a golf club, known as the European Club. There was even a race course! I saw a white man with his stick hitting a little ball; following behind was an African boy carrying the bag. One day, when I was twelve years old, I went to the gate and said, "Can I come in?" He said, "No". I said, "Can I join, if I get the money from my mum?" "You join? It's a white man's club – it's a European club!" So somebody suggested that I become an apprentice caddy. So I went back and said, "Can I be a caddy?" "Ah, now you're talking! You want to be a caddy, right?" So I became a caddy, I wanted to learn about the game. Then one day, my mum found out. Someone had seen me carrying a white man's bag and told her. My mum called me in and said, "Why are you carrying a white man's bag, what was in the bag?" I said, "Oh, it's this game called golf", "What is golf, am I not giving you enough pocket money?" I said, "No, it's not that mum, I just want to know about it, so I became a caddy." She said it was an insult to her because she was a business woman with plenty of money and I was carrying the bag of a white man. But I insisted and I was a caddy until I went to Yaba Tech.

Mr Anthony Maduagwu

I went to school in Lagos. If you did well you went up to the next class but, if you failed, you stayed behind. Sometimes there were students who were still in the same class even after pupils of their age had finished five years before! I remember we had to rush to catch the bus. If you were late for school, or if you failed to do your homework, you were punished. We respected the teachers.

I participated in lots of sports such as football and boxing. I even played for the national side. We were called the baby team because we were still young. I remember playing for the Challenge cup, the Nigerian cup, and the school cup. We didn't play any traditional African games, but I listened to traditional music such as 'High

Life', which used all sorts of wooden and metal percussion instruments.

I grew up in a very close family and I have to admit I was spoilt! As I was the first born, I didn't have to do anything. My sister did everything with my mother and my younger brother. When I used to come home from school I would leave my dirty clothes on the floor, and my mum would wash, iron and hang them up.

When I finished elementary school I went Yaba Tech engineering school. I did engineering for four years. Yaba Tech was a boarding school, and after four years I qualified. I trained to be an air conditioner and refrigeration engineer. By the time I passed, many Europeans had opened up businesses in Nigeria. They came head-hunting and selected four of us. I went to work for one of these businesses. I was lucky, even though I wasn't from a rich family, I didn't experience any hardship.

Mr James Adebayo Adesina

My sister was so much older than me that I used to think she was my mother. When I went to school and saw her there, and also my older brother, it took me by surprise. I went to the local village school which was built by my grandparents with the help of other parents. My family embraced Christianity very early on, and they built a school so that all the boys and girls in the village would not miss out on education. The teachers at my school were missionaries.

Showing how school age was determined!

They had been trained in teacher training colleges run by the mission and were posted anywhere, to villages and distant places across Nigeria, so it was the same sort of standard of education that was in the cities, sometimes even higher. The teachers were dedicated, twenty-four hours a day, almost seven days a week.

I began school at the age of seven. It is quite interesting how they determine when you are ready to go to school. I was lucky, my age was registered when I was born. But my peers didn't have that privilege so, to determine their age, the missionaries would ask each child to go in front of the teacher, and stretch his hand over his head. If the tip of his finger did not touch the ear on the other side, they were not old enough to start school! The school I went to did not discriminate against

Christians, Muslims or even pagans, they accepted everyone. If they wanted to convert to Christianity, so much the better!

We did a lot of counting, reading and what we called recitation. The teacher would recite and we would memorise. In the second year, we started reading more. We read all types of books mostly written by English authors. The books were brought by missionaries. Sometimes the books were translated into Yoruba or into other native tongues. But as time went on, in the second, third and fourth year we started to read the English language. By the time I was ten, I was writing, learning English language, English grammar, history, geography, and what we called nature study. Between the ages of fourteen and fifteen I took a 'Middle Two Certificate.' That is the general entrance exam for a grammar school. I moved from a village school to a city school, because the village school was limited.

Since I was young, I had always wanted to become a land surveyor. An interest sparked when I came into the city, and I saw people pegging houses and using chains hooked onto rods to measure them. I asked my mum what they were doing, and she said, "They are surveyors." She said, "They are trying to measure that house." And I said, "When I grow up, I want to be a surveyor." And little wonder, as I grew up, my interest developed further.

From secondary school I took up engineering. I ended up living in the city of Ibadan twenty miles from my village to continue my education, so I had to say goodbye to the village, but I did return for holidays. We had four holidays in the year. Every three months there was a break, especially during the very hot season. In the summertime, it was not easy to sit in the classroom. After I qualified, I remained in the city for nine years working for a civil engineering company. We took up contracts the length and breadth of Nigeria, and remember, it is a massive country. I missed my village but we were making progress with the railway lines and I could visit the village any time. When I was dying to see my old friends or parents, I just boarded a train to my village and stayed a day or two.

Mrs Mako Herabe

My brothers went to Koranic school from the age of six and they would get up early with my father. I didn't go to school. Girls had 'informal' schooling. I learned household duties like building a hut. I helped my mother. She would explain how to construct a hut with sticks. I also learned basket making, working with the grown ups. Around noon we stopped for second prayer, we ate some lunch, then continued working. All the family came together at sunset.

In the evening we had a big dinner of ugali, which is made up of grain and corn. We also prepared some stew of meat, but we mostly drank milk because there was plenty of it. After dinner, the elders would tell ghost and horror stories. I didn't stay up too late, as I had to wake up early.

Mrs Hawa Ismail Mumin
I did not go to school. During the day all the boys and girls played together, we didn't have anywhere to go. I remember a couple of games we used to play. When it rained we made sand castles and competed with each other to see who could make the biggest one. We also played a stick game called 'Lal'. This game was a bit like rugby, you had two teams that would play against each other. The stick was thrown into the air and whoever caught it aimed for the goal. The opposite team had to stop that player from scoring. We didn't have prizes or cups to give away, the losers' forfeit was to carry the winners on their backs to their huts. One of my other favourite games was 'Kowton' which is a bit like Jacks or Fivestones. You created a dip in the sand, placed shells in there and threw them up and caught them on the back of your hand – both boys and girls played these games.

CARIBBEAN ELDERS

Mrs Irma Reid
I started school when I was five, in San Fernando. My brother went to a boys' Roman Catholic school and my sister and

Irma's family – Irma is on the right

I went to a girls' Roman Catholic school. My routine for school was having a shower and then getting ready. My mother would plait my hair every day. In school we used a black slate and we either used chalk or a slate pencil to write with. I always liked spelling and English and I was awarded lots of prizes.

We didn't help Mum around the house when we were little, but as we got older we used to do a lot more. She used to do embroidery and crochet and we would sit in the gallery with her. She used to tell us wonderful stories. I really looked forward to night-time. She was very imaginative and I think she made these stories up herself, because I have never seen them written down anywhere. She also used to sing songs. Weekends were a time for family outings. My father would take us to the beach or a drive down to the country. I know my Dad used to go dancing. He loved dancing and I think, before Mum had us, she used to go dancing with him. My father always commented how my mother was such a good dancer.

My mum was a Roman Catholic, but my dad was Church of England. My dad was always insistent that we go to church. We always went to mass on Sunday. Mass was an hour long, we had to dress properly and you had wear a veil on your head or a skull cap and girls were certainly not allowed to wear trousers in church then. I was part of the Catholic Youth Organisation and they always organised dances. As I got older I was allowed to stay out longer, but we had to be home by 10pm. My father was still strict, even up until the time I decided to leave and come over here. We used to go to what we called 'Dutch' parties, where you took a bottle and some food.

I always wanted to be a nurse. I remember writing an essay about it, and how I wanted to travel to Europe and study nursing. Another girl in my class wrote a similar essay on the same theme and we both got into trouble because the teacher thought we copied from one another, but we hadn't. Margaret ended up going to the States and working in an office. I eventually came to England and did nursing. But I had to fight with my

dad first. He knew I wanted to be nurse and he knew I always wanted to come to England but he wasn't keen on that. He wanted me train in Trinidad. He was worried about me, and found the thought of my leaving home very daunting. Also, back then, it was very expensive to fly, so you had to travel by boat, and he heard rumours about how sailors carried on.

Mrs Gladys Smith

I attended an Anglican school. I am a Methodist but I never went to a Methodist school. I went to school until I was sixteen. I then did one year's training to become a teacher. We learned the basics at school, such as addition, subtraction, multiplication and division. As you grew older, you changed from one class to the next, but we didn't have a teacher for every subject. We did a bit of history, a bit of geography, a bit of English. English was in two sections: grammar and literature.

My favourite subject was English. I always wanted to speak correct English because I did English grammar and I loved to say the right thing at the right time. I am happy that I can hold my own with anybody when it comes to speaking properly. I haven't had any special training; I just did it on my own! My father spoke very well and was very strict. At home we were not bound to hard and fast rules, but if you didn't say something correctly, he might say, "Oh, that doesn't sound right!" I loved reading Shakespeare, and English composition. I didn't enjoy history because of remembering dates. We did British Empire history. We were taught about kings and queens and the dates of their reigns. We learned about different governments, prime ministers' names and the most outstanding events of that time.

Empire Day was just the greatest day for a school child. We all looked forward to it, when we wore new uniforms or a new dress. We all dressed in white, or the uniform of the school. Not all schools had one. It was a children's celebration and we looked forward to the treat which was a drink and a bun! That meant so much to us, we had ginger beer – homemade of course – and a bun, that was wonderful!

Mr Michael Roper

I was a brilliant student! I remember at the age of three or four, all the women used to gather at my house and listen to me read. I used to read the pink society pages in the magazines. The women wanted to know what was happening and I would read every word. As my reward for reading, I was given chocolate! All the women fussed over me and spoiled me. My mother wasn't pleased about that, she thought it made me more naughty.

I started infant school at the age of four. It was privately run by a lady who also ran the local shop and she taught me to read fluently. I then went to an elementary school. Walking to school was an ordeal, as I had to cross very busy roads always full with traffic. My mother had to go to work, so she paid a boy to walk me to school. When I first joined the school, they were not aware of my talents so I was put in the lower class, but by lunchtime I was put in the higher class. My favourite teacher was Miss Johnson. She thought I was a bright pupil. I was really good at exams and always came top. I did feel out of place, because all the other children in my class were much bigger than me. I remember the older boys didn't like me, but the girls were friendly because the boys were knocking me about. The girls called them "dead beats". I was very good at doing sums and geography. I knew all the countries in the world.

When I was approaching seven, my mother took me out of the school. I went to a strict Catholic school where I was taught by the nuns. I got hit with a ruler once because my hands were dirty. There was one sister who was really strict, her name was Sister Michael and she always called me 'vile demon'. At the age of nine, I played for the school football team. One day, I was kicking the ball as usual, when a lady passed by with some fruit in a basket. The ball dropped and knocked the basket over. She took the ball. I went up to her and said, "Excuse me, you are stopping the game and it is our play time". She put the ball in the basket. The ball was in the middle of the basket, so I leapt up to get it and of course the whole basket came tumbling down. No one could run as fast as me. My father used to call me the 'black breeze'! When I got back to school, Sister Michael was standing outside the gate. She said, "Boys, I hope you have your lunch money because you are going to pay for the damaged goods". So she started walking around the class, and collected the money and paid the woman.

After school I went to St Jarvis College to study electrical engineering. I wasn't sure exactly what I wanted to do, but my father nicknamed me 'flash' because I could build a sound system out of spare parts. So during college I fixed appliances and electrical goods. I remember building a radio when the Indians came to play cricket. I built a radio from nothing. I started knocking up more radios. I built a transmitter, with a needle from a record player. With the signal from the radio, I broadcasted where I lived. So the guys used to come and say 'play this tune for me', 'play that tune for me'. People started paying me for playing tunes, I became a popular guy. Then one-day a big black policeman (we called him 'hateful man' because he didn't like boys) was walking up my road. He came up to me and asked me what I was doing. He said, "Listen, I don't like this kind of thing, because, you are interfering with post office equipment. I don't want to hear anymore about it. You are not allowed to broadcast from this area." He then got a stick and he went BANG! He destroyed everything. He said to me, "Listen, you'd better stop or I will haul you to jail. Do not make any more of these things". So I didn't make anymore.

ASIAN ELDERS

Mrs Avtar Bilkhu

I went to nursery and then to elementary school. My school was very close to my home. At that time they were no chairs and desks; we had to sit on the floor. We wrote on a piece of slate. I was taught Punjabi and Hindi. After the fifth class I learned a little bit of English. When I got to the eighth class I took up maths, history and English. In the tenth class, I learned geography and physiology. I then went to study at Ramgarhia College, Phagwara, which was not far from my village, I used to cycle there everyday. I finished college at 19.

I really wanted to be a doctor, but my mother fell ill with cancer. I had to take care of her and, at that time, both my father and uncle were planning my marriage. I had passed all my exams, but I was told to stay at home and look after my mum. My elder sister was living in Ludhiana and came to help me. I spent most of my time indoors being a full time carer. The pressure of marriage was partly due to the people in my village who thought I needed to settle down.

Mr Fazal Rahim Shah

My father's job in the police service meant we didn't stay at one school, but moved around a lot. It was hard moving from one school to the next, but we got used to it,

Mr Fazal Shah's father in uniform

because the basic education system is the same all over the country. Sometimes, if we were in the middle of exams when there was a move planned, my father would leave us for two or three months in a hostel to finish our studies. I don't know whether you would call it exciting or not, but now I realise that moving around and mixing with different people enriched my life. That's why, if somebody talks about a town, I say, "Yes, I know it", and people are surprised that I have heard of it.

My college education was in Lahore and we ended up settling there. My parents brought a very big house. At that time my

father had become a high-ranking officer, so he didn't have to move around as much. I finished my studies in 1959, and in 1960 I came here. All my brothers went on to do really well: one became a police officer, the eldest was a veterinary surgeon – he's retired now – and the third one was a film sound engineer. I was the maverick of the family. I wanted a totally different life. I didn't know what I wanted to do, but I knew I didn't want to be a police officer. I'd seen how hard my father worked – no time off, no holidays. I don't remember my father taking us shopping. Always working, all the time, day and night… work!

My father was a hockey player. He was very good. He was so good that he was on the verge of representing India in the Olympics. He brought up all four of us brothers playing hockey with him. So in one team it was five of us – four sons and one father. We never had time to go to the pictures, just playing hockey with the boys. We came from school, did our homework, and went to the field to play hockey. By the time we were finished it was dark and we were tired. I was playing very good hockey at 18, and then while I was in university. When I moved here I played international hockey. All my brothers were playing as well. Hockey was the main thing, and even at the age of forty-two, I played here.

Mr Bagwant Singh

As a child I went to school in Moshi in Tanzania. This was only for a short period because my dad moved with his job to different stations. My school in Moshi was mixed, but we mostly grew up with Sikh and Gujarati communities, so I learned to speak and write Gujarati. I think when we were in fifth or sixth form we learned English. I could also speak Swahili, but now I have forgotten most of it. My favourite subject at school was art. I was really good at it and I used to enjoy singing as well.

Every five years, my father used to go back to India for six months at a time and visit his parents. He used to work for five years without having any holiday, so then he could save it up for these longer visits. When I was 16, my father decided to take me to India, because we couldn't get a proper education in Africa as we were travelling around all the time. The whole family went to India for a holiday.

We travelled to India by ship, which was really big. I remember how we played on the deck. We were travelling in economy class with other Asians who were working people. It took fifteen days to travel from East Africa to India, depending on the weather. My mum used to get up in the morning and cook on the stove. We docked at Bombay and then we caught the train to Punjab. We stayed in Amritsar and then from Amritsar we moved to Jalandhar. My parents returned back to Africa with my younger siblings and I remained behind in India with two brothers and two sisters. I was very sad about leaving Africa because it was such a good place. Even now, I have seen so many countries, but there is nowhere like Africa, it is so beautiful.

I stayed in Jalandhar for fifteen to sixteen years. At first we didn't stay with family; we stayed in a girls' hostel and my brothers and I were the only boys! My father's family lived close by, so we didn't feel alone. We knew we were there to study and we had a guardian who took good care of us. I think after a year and half my mum came back with the rest of the family and bought a house. We all moved from the hostel and stayed with my mum, but my father still had to go back to Africa and finish his service. He worked from 1926 to1963, and he retired in 1964.

In India I studied a BA in music. After I finished my studies I started working. I set up my own little business. I employed a few people, but I still continued my studies in the evenings. I used to work very hard, I got up at five o'clock. My job was in engineering. We had a lathe and machines and we manufactured parts. I wanted to learn more, so I thought I would come to England.

Mrs Pramila Desai
Normally girls were not encouraged to be educated that highly because parents wanted them to get married. The community couldn't understand why my dad encouraged me. But my family wanted me to go to school. My father believed in education for boys and girls. My brothers went to a special school which cost a lot more money than mine and they were more educated than me, but everyone was educated in my family. Most families found it hard, as money either had to be saved for marriage or put towards schooling.

I liked going to school. I had plenty of friends. Schools were located near the house, because families were protective over girls, and were worried that something might happen. I had to get up for school at 9 o'clock and I used to get home about 5 o'clock. I used to come home for lunch because my school was so near. I would have chapattis, rice and dhal.

I studied in the Gujarat school for the first seven years. It was a mixed school and all my classes were taught in Gujarati. Then I went to an English school in 1955. I was lucky because I was awarded a scholarship for my place at the English

JS High School, Sojitra, 1956 – Pramila is seated front row, second from right

school. Only three people got a scholarship in my village. The scholarship was given to children with disability or if you passed your exams.

We used to do lots of exercise. I was a champion in sport, I really liked exercises and wrestling. I used to get a lot of prizes like a book or pencils. I remember winning a race where I held a matkhi (storage pot) full of water and ran; another race was putting a spoon in my mouth with a lemon balancing on the spoon, a bit like egg and spoon. I was really into sports and so were my brothers and sisters; they all had medals as well.

After a day of school, I did my homework. Then I helped my mother and sister with domestic chores. After that I would meet up with friends and chat, knit and devise competitions. As a young girl I was able to move round freely, as long as I helped with chores and participated in celebrations and rituals like fasting for five days, doing whole nights where we could sit down and talk.

On the whole my childhood was really great, but I was also quite ill. I had diabetes from when I was born. I enjoyed life, but sometimes I was very tired and ill. At that time in India my family and I didn't know it was diabetes. My skin used go patchy and spotty, but we didn't know what was wrong with me. They only knew I had diabetes after I was married and lost my first baby. The doctor made a diagnosis.

I always had the dream of doing a job.

A 'matkhi' storage pot

I always wanted to work. I remember there was a vacancy in the village library, so I worked there for three months. I was about 14 or 15 and I didn't get paid much money because it was very small and they couldn't really afford it, but I did it more for the experience.

Growing Up
Creative Activities

OLDER PEOPLE'S ACTIVITIES

'Rule Britannia'

So many story-tellers speak about a schooling based on British patterns. Note how much they concentrated on the history, literature and geography of Great Britain and how many of their teachers were educated according to the British system. Was this equally true for the members of the group? If so, how did this affect their attitudes to the 'mother country'? Do they feel it was right to have this very British education? What were the gains and losses resulting from it?

We Learned by Heart

What songs and poems did the older people learn by heart at school? Have a half hour of recitation, writing down or tape-recording all the poems remembered. Extend this activity to remembered times-tables and other measures of weight, distance, volume, etc.

Once Upon A Time

Do the group members remember stories told them as children by their parents and grandparents at home or by their teachers at school? Can they re-tell favourite stories to one another, seeing how common the characters and situations are from one culture to another and where the significant differences lie.

In My School Bag

Pass round an old fashioned school satchel and ask everyone in the group to pretend to put in it something they remember taking to school. They should say what it is as they put it in, and they can add a little explanation where necessary.

A Message to My Teacher

If members of the group could go back and speak to their teachers, what would they like to say to them. How have their lives been influenced by these teachers? Do they still remember injustice in the classroom? Do they feel grateful for the knowledge and skills their teachers gave them? Try playing out this imaginary meeting with a remembered teacher in pairs, and then reverse the roles. The person playing the 'teacher' should listen, but does not necessarily need to say anything. The 'pupil' can speak as an adult looking back, and does not have to speak as a child.

Sticks & Carrots

Ask members of the group to talk about the prizes they won and the punishments they received. These memories can be played out by the group, with everyone having an opportunity to see their 'scene' performed.

Games We Played

How many people in the group remember the games they played as children? Try out some of these games with home-made toys which can be constructed by the group and compare with other group members the rules and regulations of the games. This is an enjoyable activity to extend to young people, so that inter-generational comparisons can be made.

When I Grew Up I Wanted To Be...

What were the ambitions of the group members when they were young? Did they want to continue their education beyond the level available locally? What kinds of obstacles were put in their way? Examples might be financial restrictions, parents' need for help in the home or workplace, parents' fear of over-educating their daughters, lack of suitable educational facilities locally, or just prejudice.

Far From Home

Many of the men were sent away for education and began to lose touch with their home and community. Was this the case for some of the group members? If so, how did it affect their attitude to travel abroad later on?

Let's Celebrate

If the group consists of people from different backgrounds, it might be interesting to make a list of all the religious festivals celebrated and look for images which show how they are observed with special foods, costumes and ceremonies. Members of the group might enjoy explaining their favourite festivals to one another, whether as remembered from childhood and youth, or as practiced today.

The Role of Religion in My Life

Religion played a big part in the lives of many of the storytellers. Was attendance at church, temple, or other place of worship an important part of the 'growing up' years of members of the group? Was it something they looked forward to, or

Chinese New Year celebrations, at the Broadway Theatre, Lewisham 2004

was it just an obligation, something which was expected of them? How far have members of the group continued to practice the religions of their childhood? Has it been a source of strength and comfort to them in their lives? Do they feel that religious observance is still sufficiently strong in the communities they live in today? Have their children and grandchildren continued to observe religious practices?

YOUNG PEOPLE'S ACTIVITIES

School Photo

Look at the photographs in this book which have been supplied by the older people of their school days, and notice how similar they are to the British equivalents at the time. Ask for grandparents and great-grandparents' photos and bring them in to compare.

Discipline & Punishments

Find out from your grandparents or an older neighbour how teachers punished children in the past. Compile a list of all the 'crimes and punishments' you have heard about and then compare what happens today in your classroom.

It's Not Fair

Many of the women had less schooling than their brothers. Those who did progress well and wanted to obtain qualifications often had to forget their own careers to look after sick parents, younger siblings, or to get married. Compare this with your own situation. Can you imagine what it would be like for brothers and sisters to be treated completely differently? Working in groups, prepare a scene in which a daughter asks to be allowed to go to school, and the parents have to argue the case for only educating the boys. Try to enter into the culture of the family you are representing and the feelings of the daughter in questioning the existing pattern of behaviour.

Helping at Home

Notice how many people had to work in the fields or in the home to help their parents, often after a day's schooling. What are you expected to help with and how do you feel about it? Are girls and boys expected to help out equally? Draw up lists of tasks undertaken by class members and compare those done by boys and girls.

Then & Now

Very large families meant that mothers were working hard all the time, cooking, washing, sewing, shopping for food or growing their own food. Most of this work was done by hand with no kitchen appliances or sewing machines. Can you think how many labour-saving devices have been introduced since those days which have transformed a mother's working day? You can come right up to date with internet shopping. Make a list of all the changes you can think of.

Mums Then & Now

Smaller families and labour-saving domestic appliances have radically altered women's lives and ambitions. Compare your mother's life with two of the descriptions of mothers' lives offered in this chapter. Make up 'a day in the life of...' and see how many differences there are, including the possibilities for paid employment outside the home, leisure, education and sporting opportunities for today's mothers.

Games & Toys Exchange

Invite some older people, perhaps grandparents or great grandparents from different ethnic backgrounds to share with you their memories of the games they played as children. Then explain the games which delight children today and demonstrate to the elders how they are played. There may be songs attached to games, like skipping rhymes. Compare these with the ones the elders sang, and learn each other's songs.

Many older people remember playing with homemade toys and they may have made toys for their own children and grandchildren in the traditional way. Invite them into the classroom to show you how they did this and show them the toys you play with and where you buy them. Making a kite and learning to fly it can be an enjoyable joint activity.

Sheila Rakhit in India with her first radio

The World Before Television

Most people in this chapter remember playing with friends in the open air, at sports and games, swimming in the sea and racing games on the sand. Others played indoor games or did sewing and other craft work. Remember that computers and television were not available to our story-tellers when they were young. What difference would it make to your life if suddenly there was no television and no computers? What do you think you might do with your free time? Would you see it as a tragedy or an opportunity? Write five sentences to explain how you spend your evenings after school now, and put a star by the ones which would not have applied to the storytellers in this chapter.

Chapter Three: Courtship & Marriage

CHINESE ELDERS

Mr Ke Wing Pang

I got married in 1958 when I was about 24. It was organised through matchmakers. There were professional matchmakers, and some that were just people we knew, but mine was a proper matchmaker. My wife-to-be lived in a neighbouring village, her family were farmers as well. The matchmaker went to both houses to discuss the potential suitors. If the girl is interested, then the matchmaker returns to let the parents know. Once that is agreed, everybody goes out for lunch together. We were sitting side-by-side, but she was very shy and so was I so we didn't say much to each other or eat much either. When we returned home, my parents asked me what I thought, but because my family was poor and didn't have any money, you just don't have a lot of choice. So we both agreed to the marriage.

Engagement involves many rituals. What happens is the girl must write her name, date of birth and the time of birth on a red piece of paper in black ink and this is then handed to my family. The paper is put on the altar. This bit of paper represents her; it is a bit like a contract. The groom doesn't have to do this; it is only done by the bride. After placing the paper on the altar, we have to light three joss sticks and put them in an incense pot. What happens is, if one of them stops lighting, or if they don't all burn down together, that means the girl is not suitable. This ritual goes on for three days. We have to hope nothing bad happens or nothing gets broken in the house. So if nothing goes wrong in the house this means she is suitable and that she won't bring bad luck. Luckily for me the joss sticks all burnt down. After that we have to collect information on my birthday and time of birth and the girl's birthday and her time of birth, and then they go to a soothsayer to see how we will match. If the chart says it is okay, then it's okay. It is quite a long process, but once it is fine then the matchmaker will inform the girl's family. In the Chinese tradition, when it is okay, they will talk about the dowry, not from the girl's side, but from the man's side. They will then ask the matchmaker to see what the girl's family want. For the engagement we give biscuits and roast pork and other things and money. The biscuits and pork are distributed amongst family and friends. We then set a date for an official engagement.

Another special ritual takes place. We can't just marry at anytime; we must go to the tailors and get our clothes made, so it can't just be a rushed job; the outfit has to be properly cut and made. The tailor is chosen by the person who reads out birth charts. They will inform us who will make those wedding dresses. There is even a time given for the tailor to cut the cloth. The cloth must be cut exactly at the time suggested by the astrologer. It could be midnight or two in the morning; a different time, depending on her and him. Yes, the first cut of the cloth has to be at that time. However you can never be too sure that the tailor will cut it at the exact time. He could just say, "Yeah I will cut it," but he might not, so we give them a red packet with money in it. I suppose it is a bit of a bribe! My wedding suit was a silk jacket with a mandarin collar, black with a green lining and I wore black trousers with it. Up until this point I hadn't really seen my bride-to-be. It was all done through the matchmaker.

On the morning of the wedding, the priest arrived to carry out the prayer. In my case, we had to fetch my fiancée from her village in China. Although it was quite near, in fact just across the river from the part of New Territories, Hong Kong, where I was living, we needed to have special official papers for this.

Once the bride arrives at the house, we have a dinner or feast at about six o'clock, before the ceremony takes place. All the girls are in one room and they sing and play games with the bride. After that, the bride and groom pray to the altar. Then we have another party and that is when the men tease the wife. Teasing involves playing pranks embarrassing the bride

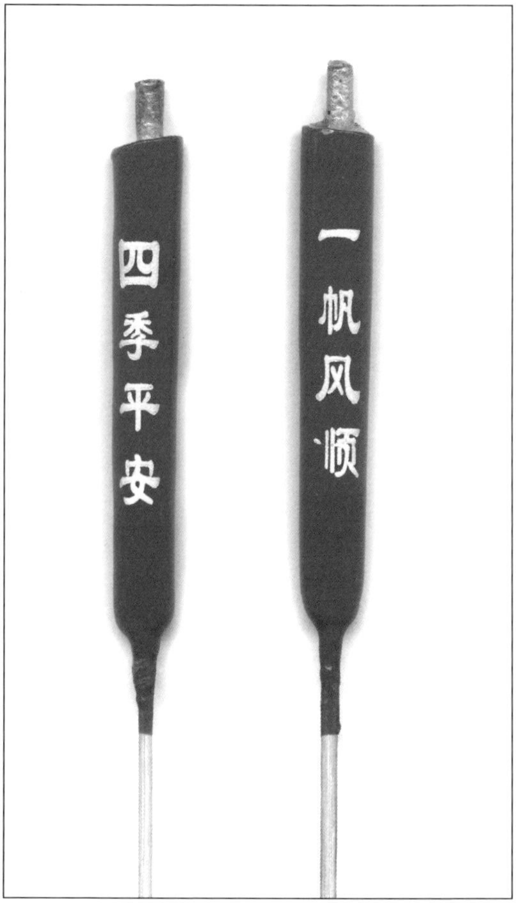

and groom. Like tying an apple with a string and somebody holds it in the middle and both husband and wife will try and have a bite of the apple. Sometimes we either cut a slice of apple or orange or someone gets the husband and wife to feed each other. Then the friends will pay mahjong, and the husbands will be in the room with the wife. At about eleven o'clock the wife will come down and cook dinner for us.

The next part of the ceremony, which is after the teasing, we pray to the gods and the ancestors – that is the wedding ceremony. What happens is, after eleven o' clock, we have two red Chinese candles on a stick and we light the candles and we have two cups of tea and traditional candies. These are taken to the bride and groom's bedroom. There is one for the man and one for the woman. Finally we end with Chinese crackers. By midnight everybody leaves.

The groom's teasing by the bride's family begins the next day with lots of jokes and songs and this can go on for over twenty nights. It doesn't happen all day; it begins around ten o'clock and finishes about midnight. The duration of teasing can determine how popular you are. If people don't come and tease you, people say you don't have a lot of friends. At the wedding, if the parents see a lot of guests then they are happy.

As my family house only had one main bedroom, my father and mother went away to stay with someone else, so we could have the house to ourselves. The next morning, you have to kneel down and give tea to your elders. Each one will be given a cup of tea. On the third day, the girl goes back to her parent's house, and then on the same day, she returns back to the groom's house. After this, the house belongs to the groom and his parents live close by.

Mrs Ah Poh Luong

I was married at 19. It is not like now, where you can go and meet your husband. You are introduced and told to marry. It is not up to us to choose. My husband was not one of the boat people. He came from Hai Phong, which was a French colony, a busy town full of very big shops. By the time I was 19, all my brothers and sisters were married; I was the youngest. A match-maker, who was sent on behalf of the boy, arranged my marriage. I didn't even see him. It is up to the parents to decide whether he is a good boy; then they will allow it. If not, then they don't.

The marriage took place in my village. The day started off with having tea with the elders. Then there was a large feast with plenty of meat and fish. We ate and celebrated, and then they came and fetched me in a boat and took me to my husband's family. We then prayed to the elders, the deceased ones, and then they brought me back to my boat. I was wearing a Chom Sung which was made up of a long black skirt and a blue blouse. The wedding went on for most of the day. I then left my father's boat and headed to his relatives' house for another feast. Then the next day we head back to Hai Phong. I wasn't really sad about leaving my family. They were still quite near; about four hours boat ride from Hai Phong, so I could go back at anytime.

My husband, Lowa, worked in a shop

in Hai Phong. I lived with his family. He managed a warehouse which stored goods brought in by ship, and he dealt with the paperwork. Sometimes my husband had to go on the boats. If the company asked him to, he had to go with the boat to Hong Kong to deliver the goods. It was a sort of import-export business; they do potatoes, onions and things like that. From the big steamers they would take the goods onto the shore. I remember when I was living in Hai Phong seeing many French people. They mainly had the big shops selling materials and vegetables and fruits. I didn't really know them very well, but a lot of the French did know Vietnamese and Cantonese so they could converse with us.

I stayed at home and took care of the home and did the shopping. I didn't know anybody in the town and all my family were still living on the boats. Occasionally we would go to the cinema and sometimes we went for Chinese Dim Sum. I lived in Hai Phong until I left Vietnam. By that time, I had four children. There were two girls, two boys. But about four or five others died of illnesses. My children had a very different life to me. I encouraged my daughters to go to school.

Mrs Phuong La

After a year in Macao, I travelled with my sister and her husband to China. I was 20. Because of the war, the money did not have any value. My brother-in-law opened up a laundry, but it didn't do that well, so my sister, her husband and children went back to Hong Kong. But I stayed behind because by this time I was married.

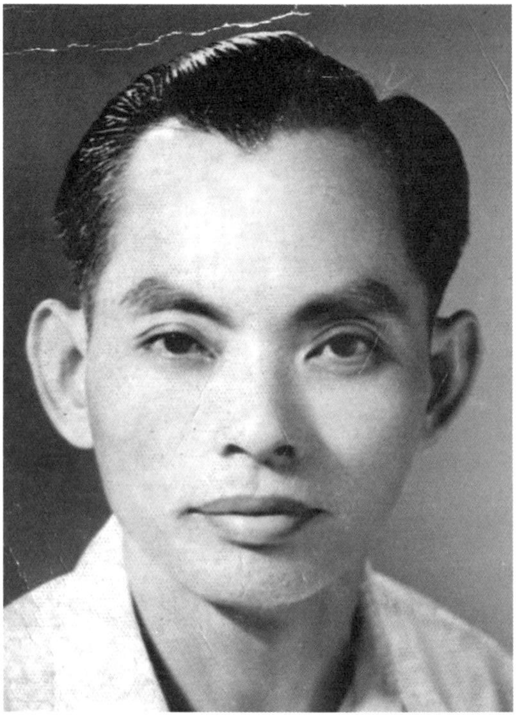

Mrs La's husband...

I met my husband whilst I was working in the cigarette factory. He worked there too but he dealt with the administration side of the cigarette factory. We got to know each other, he approached my sister and we got married. We didn't have a big wedding; all we did was advertise it in the papers, and that's how we married, because it was still the war time and it was cheaper to advertise. The advertisement worked as a marriage certificate. I said my name, he

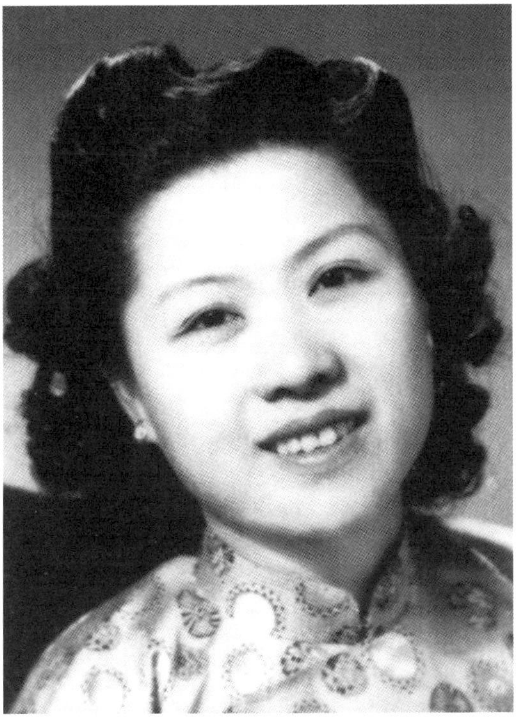

...and Mrs La herself, as a young wife

said his and we were married. We then had a wedding dinner with my sister-workers from the factory and some family.

We left China for Vietnam in 1945. The factory opened up a branch in Vietnam and we were sent there; there were 20 of us. We used to be given 20 cigarettes a day; that's how I learn to smoke and still do. My first daughter was born in Vietnam, I had two children by the time I was 28.

Mrs Mooi Tran

I was 21 when I got married. It was all arranged by parents. Someone approached my parents and they went to see the prospective groom. I had no say. My parents didn't care so much about what the prospective son-in-law did for a living. The most important thing for them was that he respected the elders and was gentle; those were the main criteria. Once they had seen him, they told me, and it was arranged. I had to accept my parents' wishes. The groom's family gives you and your friends biscuits. We were also asked how much we wanted for the wedding from the groom's family. After the dowry has been agreed, then both sides will celebrate and have individual feasts. We are then engaged and a week passes until the wedding day.

I didn't see the groom until the wedding day. The wedding began in the morning. My parents gathered my friends and we celebrated together. In those days, three or four days before the wedding, there would have been many feasts; my mother and father would have invited many people. They would have had roast pork and duck, loads of nice food to entertain friends. I had two different outfits for the wedding; the first was a red top and skirt with intricate embroidery, but when I was at the groom's house later on, I changed into a traditional Chinese wedding dress with a head-dress and presented myself to my in-laws. I had to kneel down and offer tea to them.

They decorated the car with lots of flowers made into bouquets and there was music and singing. My mother employed people to go with me in the car. They showed me how to offer tea to the in-laws. My parents didn't go with me; I had to go by myself. I was very nervous. I didn't know what to expect. I had never left my parents until now so I was scared going to a complete stranger's house. When I reached the groom's house, a woman came and gave me a piggy-back into the groom's house. This was the first time I actually saw him. On the third day the tradition is to go back to your parents where I was fed roast pig. Then later on my husband came and picked me up.

I had a very traditional marriage. My husband went out to work and I looked after the home and family. I had four boys, no girls. I was still living in the city, but kept myself to myself. My husband was very busy running the restaurant, while I took care of the boys, got them ready for school and visited my parents. I didn't live on my own though. I had servants to help me take of the home and my in-laws were there too. I hardly saw my husband as he took more interest in earning money. I would take the boys and visit him at the restaurant.

Mrs Makfung San

I had an arranged marriage when I was twenty-five years old. I had never seen my husband before, although we lived in the same city. I wore a Chinese traditional wedding dress, and a big Chinese hat with a veil covering the face. The groom's family had to pay quite a lot of money to my family. A certain amount of gold, a certain amount of money, a certain amount of pig!

At the beginning, even knowing that I had to marry him, I liked him. I thought, yes, he's quite good looking! He's okay! I lived with his family, together, in the same house. I was very happy there, although I missed my mother and father. My husband was a metal worker. He had a shop in Tong Tang, with a forge and the shop made steel work and metal work.

We had a total of seven children, but two died when they were young. When I was about forty-five years old, my husband died. He was just overworked, and at that time, we had no hospital – no doctor. When my husband died, the children were aged 1, 3, 5, 7, and the oldest was 12, so they weren't able to work. Since then, I've been single. All my children went to school. Both the boys and girls went to school in Tong Tang. I only looked after the kids at home. I was a housewife.

Mrs Suk Tsang Tang

When I was 27 years old, I married a photographer in Vietnam. He had a shop in Saigon for people to come in for family portraits. Not everybody had a camera in those days, so if you wanted a family picture, you would have to go this shop. We had two sons and two daughters.

Mrs Josephine Macpeppele Ja Ja

I was 16 when I left school and got married. What happened was that they would put you in the 'fattening house'. If you are skinny, the older women feed you three times a day. Some of them are family and some of them are neighbours. They rub some red tints on your body to make your skin fine, then they'll bath you, scrub you well and keep you clean. They also teach you how to care for your husband; so that when he comes home you don't start talking at him immediately, you ask him how his work was, and cool him down, because he has met many many people. You don't know who may have offended him; so you calm him down. Then after that, you bring him food. Or if he wants a bath, you wash him before eating. If he says he'll eat before bathing, it's okay.

You stayed in the fattening house for up to two or three months. During that time, you only talked to the girls; if you went out and talked to boys, you were in trouble. You didn't go out, except in the night because other people won't see you in the dark.

At the end of the time, the men carried gifts for the bride. And the gifts they gave us were clothes wrapped up and put into a special box and a crown for the bride. The elders would check the things. They would

count the clothes, and if they were not correct, the men would have to buy more before the box could be taken and approved. Then they made an arena in the centre of the village where all the girls and older women would come and sing for you and dance. If you don't dance yourself, you will pay a fine, because the women have been teaching you indoors to dance, and now the day has come when you must show what you have learned and the people will watch you. People would pass you money when they see that you dance well. Your husband would see you when you danced. Then, after that dancing, in the night, the women led you to the husband's place, carrying the box of gifts.

The bride would wear the crown and the special clothing on the Saturday night before the wedding and on Sunday we would go to church. Four big strong hefty men would carry you there on a special chair, one holding each leg of the chair. And when you reach the church they remove the crown. The marriage is blessed and the couple sign the book. Then there is another party where the couple sit down with all the guests, and everybody dances and feasts.

The whole marriage was arranged through my parents, especially my mother. After the wedding, I lived with my husband's family. It was only about two houses away from my daddy. I was the only child of my mother, so my family didn't want me to go too far away. I was only 16 years old and they wanted me safe and close by. My mother-in-law was always kind to me.

But then, in 1956, I went to Lagos with my husband. He worked in the railway office there. I had my first child, a daughter in 1957, then in 1958 I had a second one, the second daughter. Then in 1960, during the independence, I had my first son. In 1961, I had my second son. Then in 1963 my husband came to England, so I came to join him that same year, and I didn't go back to Nigeria until 1974.

Mr Ade Aderogba

I went to an all boy's boarding school, so meeting members of the opposite sex was virtually impossible. But quite often, during inter-school sports, girls came in from Queens College, or Regan Memorial Grammar School or from other Colleges. And they had to change in the boys' shower room in the boarding house. As a school prefect, I had the responsibility to marshal my boys, to make sure that they behaved. They were like lions in a cage. They'd want to see the girls, so they would say, "Sir prefect, can I go to the toilet?" And I would say, "No you can't, the girls are changing." That kind of leadership role (where you just had to be whiter than white so to speak!) made it difficult to start a dating relationship with any member of the opposite sex. So I did not have any serious relationships with women until I came to England. A lot of my colleagues who settled in England had girlfriends back home, so the moment they settled down, they sent letters, saying they would arrange passports and so on, for their spouses join them, but I was a free agent!

I met my wife on a total blind date. I was a local government officer in Camden, in St Pancras Town Hall, and my future wife was an officer in Holborn, Camden. The local Government Tennis Tournament was held in London annually those days, in the mid-sixties. I didn't have a mixed doubles partner and neither did she, and

we were drawn to play together. We met at Haverstock Hill Tennis Club, and we started playing the tournament and from there we got to know each other and ended up as boyfriend and girlfriend. I went and stayed in a town called Retford in Nottinghamshire, when we were courting. I met her parents and they were wonderful. That contributed a lot to my decision to set up a permanent relationship with this lady. They made me feel at home during the time we spent at Nottingham. So we started planning marriage and then we got married in March 1967. It was a typical Town Hall wedding with her friends from the local authority offices in Holborn and my colleagues from Saint Pancras Town Hall, my Nigerian friends and so on. We then set up home together.

It was a mixed marriage which was a rarity in those days. I remember when I went to Retford, which is a very small town, children coming out and shouting, "Black man, black man!" Some of them came to touch me. They touched my skin, and I remember one day when we sat in the park, one of them came up and touched my hair; they just couldn't resist the temptation to see what my hair felt like.

Yes, there were minor objections from both sides. One of her sisters said, "Can't you find an English man to marry? Why do you want to marry a foreigner or a black person?" And I remember one of my own brothers saying, "Why do you want to marry a foreigner? Can't you find a Nigerian in London? We can find one here, in Lagos or in Ibadan for you!" So those are things that we just took for granted, but we were both old enough to know that we were in love and that we wanted one another and had made up our minds to get married. But my mother was very supportive and so were her parents.

Mr Anthony Maduagwu

Being a Catholic I used to be scared of girls! I was a sociable being, but I was quite different from the majority of people, being very religious, and I never had a girlfriend. People thought I was going to be a Reverend Father, a priest. Even when I came to Britain, I just kept myself to myself. I never had any intimacy until I was about thirty years old. The friend I shared a house with had a girlfriend and one day, she brought a friend down with her and that's how I met my future wife and how our interest in each other developed. Eventually we got married here in London. First we had a registry office wedding and then a Catholic marriage ceremony in church. It was a good atmosphere.

Mr James Adebayo Adesina
I met my wife when I was posted to a town called Oyan, which was in Osun State in Nigeria, to construct a health centre. I met her through her cousin, who was a friend of mine. The cousin wanted to come and see me with his own girlfriend, who happened to be the classmate of my wife in the secondary teacher training college. So I visited my now wife in the school where she was teaching. And that is how we started our love affair. I was 26 when I met Janet. Back then, in the good old days, we had a set of rules in courting. You exchanged letters, all sorts of flowery letters – 'the golden key of my heart' and so on. Writing letters! And you could hold hands. People can see you doing things, but you are chaste. You don't have this intimacy while you are courting. Marriage is not taken lightly in my culture, because it is a lifetime issue. It isn't a thing where you go to the shop, you buy clothes and it doesn't fit properly so you take it back. You have this commitment for a lifetime. So all the people – family on both sides, friends on both sides – have to agree. Therefore, all the brothers and the cousins, and the relations were really involved. And that is the reason why it is not easy to get a divorce once you are married like that with the knowledge of both families. And we were both mature before we got married. I was about twenty-six, and she was about twenty-three or twenty-four, and by that time we were highly educated so we knew what we were doing.

If I were back in the village, the marriage would have been arranged very differently. Somebody from my family would have happened to know somebody from her family. And people would often initiate proceedings by saying, "I want a relation of mine to marry a relation of yours." So there was a lot of matchmaking. But apart from matchmaking, they do a lot of groundwork. If it is not somebody who knows your family very well, they will suss you out. They want to know the history of this family who are marrying the daughter or the son. What sort of family are they? They want to know their background. If they hear that the family has criminal connections or have some disease, like leprosy, then it would be, "No, you can't go there!"

Sometimes they would do a test to check on the suitability of the intended partner. Say I am a man and you are a girl and I visit you, an elderly somebody from your family will put some firewood down and take up an axe. Perhaps it's a woman of seventy or eighty and, as the boyfriend, I will not see my prospective mother-in-law or grandmother- in-law doing this hard work, so I will say, "Let me do that for you!" She says yes, then watches me do it. If, by the time I do two or three strokes, I'm getting out of breath and puffing, she'll say, "They must have some disease in that family!" But obviously if I do it in one stroke, then I am strong and healthy and okay!

In my case, by the time that the two of us agreed to marry, my family went to see her family and they gave their blessing. Having known some of the family for a long time, and some of her family having known me for a long, long time, they knew my background and there was no objection. But it took a year or two before everything was finally closed. We had the 'native' wedding there, but when I came to England it wasn't recognised so we had to have a wedding in a registry office in 1962.

Mrs Mako Herabe

I met my husband-to-be when I moved to Mogadishu. We met, then our families agreed with each other, so I was lucky. Both our families were interested because I was away from my family, so they were happy if I could get married quickly. Although my husband was working in the city, he was also from the same nomadic background as me. I was 20 when I got married. He made his living delivering goods to shops in one area where there were many Asian traders who controlled the import-export business. Whatever they imported, he delivered, so that is how he was making his living. He was living in the same area as my sister and me. We met and agreed and sent messages to the family. The two families were in the nomadic area a long way off.

The wedding took place in the city because my big sister is there and knew more about the city things, so she had the responsibility. The man's family will pay for all the expenses of the meal. The girl's family do all the arrangements, invitation, cooking, everything. He has to set up his own house and I contributed to the building of it. On the wedding day the women came together and danced, we ate sweets, killed the cow for the meat. We invited many people and we ate meat and Sor which is made of corn. After that we ate sweets which were made locally. People really enjoyed themselves. Everyone was dancing and singing but, as the bride, I had to sit and watch. The bride and groom celebrate separately. We don't exchange vows, rings or kiss. But at night time we say goodbye to everyone and we meet. I used to go to many weddings but when it was my turn I was nervous, you start panicking, worrying and all this. I had the same feeling as every girl who is getting married.

Married life meant I stopped working.

Now I had to be a house wife, so I used to cook for him and look after him until I had my first baby. However, when you are at home, you have to contribute to the family economy because it is very difficult to live on one source of income, so I didn't have to travel and do hard work but I could still make baskets and sell woven mats, while I was at home. That is what I used to do. You go to a nearby market, you sell, and you get income. He was still doing importing and exporting and making deliveries in the coastal area where we were situated, and to other people living far away.

I did visit my parents whenever we had the harvest season, or when animals were breeding very well. It was like a holiday for me to go and spend two or three months with them. I had four children, one girl and three boys. When we have a boy, we kill two goats, when we have a girl we kill one goat. There is preference for the boy because he will be responsible for the whole family, his own family and the new family that he will be building, so they always give extra. It is not a favour, but rather an extra responsibility for him, so that is what they will compensate for. Both male and female had to go for 'circumcision' at seven days old. That is when they shaved the child's head, killed a goat, gave men food and everyone was invited to celebrate. Everyone would come to read the Koran and make blessings.

I didn't got to school but my children did. They went to Koranic school from age of three. After age seven, they attend regular school, and I wanted that for them. I encouraged studying so they could have a better life, better income and a better position.

A Somalian Koranic school

CARIBBEAN ELDERS

Mrs Irma Reid

I did have a few romances back home but it was always difficult with my father being so strict. A romance did blossom at the hospital where I was a nurse. He was a patient at Hither Green Hospital. I was there for three months working on this ward. He came in with food poisoning, so that is how I met him. He was there for about a week. We sat and chatted with one another. He asked me where I was from and I used to tell him about Trinidad. Before he left the hospital, he asked me to go out with him and I said yes. Actually, I had no intention of going out with him, so when he asked me for my phone number, I just wrote down some numbers on a bit of paper and handed it to him. He rang that number and didn't have much luck, so he rang the hospital and they told him what room I was in and the phone number. I was in one of my friends' room and we were chatting and there was a knock on the door and someone said, "There is a phone call for you." So I went down to the phone. It was him and he said, "You gave me the wrong numbers." I said "Did I? I thought that I wrote the right numbers." I lied. I'm not the kind of person who just meets somebody and goes out. I was were very naïve, even though I was twenty-four by this time. It was the way we were brought up, very strict. Eventually I agreed to go out for a drink. So we went out and we were together for about 12 years. Gradually, I realised I didn't want to get married. I was too independent and I didn't actually plan to get pregnant. We talked about getting married, but we just drifted apart you know. I think once I had Victoria, our daughter, I got occupied with Victoria, he was there for her and for me and he still is if I ever need anything. We are still good friends now.

Mr Michael Roper

I remember everything about how I met my wife! I was on my way to my aunt's in Camden and I bumped into this guy who was cycling down the path. He was married to my wife's mother, but I didn't know this at the time. We got talking and went back to his place. It was strange because I dreamed of meeting my wife this way. I remember going through the park to this house in Kentish Town. I followed him in and I saw this woman sitting in the corner. I said "Wah, I had a dream about this woman!" I had been past there before, when I arranged to fix a friend's sound system, so it must have been fate that I returned there again. I introduced myself. Her name was Marjorie and we began dating.

We had a nice big wedding. There were lots people there dancing. My mother couldn't come as she was in Jamaica. After we were married, we lived in Brixton. I never returned back to Jamaica after I settled here, but I wrote to my mother and my friends all the time. My wife and I used to go to jazz clubs a lot. I remember once, we were walking up the road and she stopped the traffic, she was wearing the frock that she got married in. I'm telling you, I telling you man, she was tall, elegant and beautiful, that was my wife. We had three children, two girls and one boy. They all live in London.

Mrs May Gladys Berry

We didn't have formal proposals, like he gets down on one knee. My family decided for me and it still passes through the parents. They, or even the godparents, would be the general go-between, although the husband-to-be would choose the ring himself and I did have a nice engagement ring. The close relationship doesn't come until you get married really. But you get to talk, you spend some time together, getting to know that person you are going to marry, but you are never alone together before the marriage. There was a chaperone with you, so you could talk, but not in private. It was just the way it was and you accepted it. It is not as if you are the only person it was happening to. If you went beyond the boundaries, you were considered an outrageous girl! After the ring was presented, we had a gathering; the big party would happen after the wedding.

I wore a white dress, with a white veil and a long train. The veil was lace net, but my dress was made from a lovely material, it was trimmed with pearls. The dress was buttoned at the back. I bought my own material. It was really heavy. The bridegroom wore a suit with a flower in the buttonhole. We had lovely flowers in Jamaica. I had roses on my wedding day. We still maintain the custom of 'something old, something new, something borrowed, something blue.' I got married in 1940 when I was about 18 or 19.

A couple celebrating their wedding day

I got married in church. Not all the family could attend as they were scattered all over the island, but they sent gifts. The close relatives would come to the parish by invitation which I sent out. Weddings generally occur on a Wednesday or Sunday. Saturday is market day and people are busy rushing up and down, but on Sunday everyone is calm when they go to church. As Sunday is church day we generally get churchgoers witnessing the wedding too!

On the wedding day I was very nervous, you don't know what the crowd is like out there. But when you see faces that you know, it brightens you up. You enter the church with your father or a relative, the music is playing as you walk up the aisle, the choir is singing the bridal hymn. We don't have a best man who is in charge of the rings. A pageboy marches in front of the bride with the ring. Four bridesmaids were holding my train as I walked up the aisle. After the groom has kissed the bride we both sign the register, with two witnesses present. When we were both walking down the aisle, guests were throwing confetti and rice. Then it is time for wedding photographs. It may go in the paper if you are top notch. Once the wedding service was over, we had a big reception with a three-tiered cake and speeches. It is the bride's job to cut the cake and pass it out to all friends and families who were at the wedding. So you have to have a lot of cake. Family members who didn't attend the wedding ceremony came to the reception.

ASIAN ELDERS

Mrs Avtar Bilkhu

My family began arranging my marriage when I was 21. This was after I left college to look after my mum. Somebody approached my sister who was living in Kenya. My husband-to-be was also living in Kenya since the age of 14. He came over to India and my sister introduced me to him. His family, who lived in Jalandhar, had a very big business there. I didn't know what he looked like. I hadn't even seen any photos of him. Before our proper meeting, I met him accidentally at my sister's house when I was visiting her in Jalandhar. After he saw me the first time he asked my family if he could marry me. He never asked me anything about my education, my interests or anything. I knew he was a motor mechanic with a business in Kenya, and I thought he was very intelligent and very smart. Eight days later, we got married, we had to do it in a hurry because he didn't have enough holiday. At that time he was working for the army as a motor mechanic.

I had a Sikh wedding which took place in my village and I had to move to his parent's house near Jalandhar. I was very upset and was crying because I got married so quickly. I didn't get any chance to get used to the idea, but I didn't say anything because of my mother's illness and not wanting to upset her. I felt stuck. I couldn't say no, because at that time girls had to obey their parent's wishes. My uncle, we were very close, he was like a father, and he did ask me if I liked the boy. After 28 days of marriage my husband had to go back to Kenya. I was pregnant at the time. That time there was no family planning or anything like that. It was very difficult. My first son didn't see his father until he was two years old.

My mother was well enough for the wedding but she died after I had two children. One was five and my other son was two years old when she died. She was slowly, slowly getting worse. We had to take her to hospital in Amritsar, Jalandhar and Ludhiana. At that time, cancer was uncommon. At that time they called it 'moogli foorah.' It spread in the body. There was no medication and no cures for the different stages of cancer.

Mr Bagwant Singh

I was about thirty years old when I got married. My father by then was retired and living with us in India. All my siblings were happily married and settled so I was the only one left. My parents, with the help of a matchmaker friend of the family, chose the girl. I didn't even know that they had found a bride for me. She lived in Delhi. I was sitting at my friend's house and Father came in and gave me five rupees and said, "You have been selected. The girl lives in Delhi." Following that, the family gave me some money and Indian sweets. That's how it happened, and I would see her on the wedding day.

We travelled from Jalandhar to Delhi by train. We hired out a whole carriage and all the relatives were there and we had a party. I was really excited and then we went to Delhi and we stayed there. As we were coming from the hillside, the family made arrangements for us to stay over night. They offered us food and in the morning the wedding ceremony took place. Even during the marriage I didn't really see my wife properly because she was all covered up. The marriage took place in a temple, but I don't remember much about the place. I didn't know Delhi that well, I didn't stay there much. It was all a bit of a rush.

After the ceremony, we went for lunch. Then, when she came out, that was the first time I saw her properly. She still had the 'gungat' (veil). After the wedding we stayed over night and the celebrations continued the following day. It is not like here where all the wedding celebrations are completed within one day. We didn't travel back by train. My father had arranged for us to travel by bus. My wife and I were sitting in the front. We were really dressed up in special outfits, she was in a bride's outfit. The rest of the wedding party sat behind us. So that is how we got married. It has been thirty-five or thirty-six years now since our wedding day.

Mr Fazal Rahim Shah

I was thirty when I met my wife. I used to go back home from England every two years. When I went back in 1968, my mother started saying "if you don't marry now, maybe you will get married over there." So she pushed me to get married and arranged my marriage to a local girl who also belonged to a hockey-playing family, and they were landowners. She showed me the girl, I said okay and we got married. I stayed in India for four weeks and within these four weeks I got married and I arranged to bring my wife back with me. I went to the British Embassy, and they didn't

ask me many questions. They asked where I lived, and they gave my wife a visa. It was a lot easier then. I brought her home to England. I rented a house in Riverdale Road in Lewisham. I had a few friends here, a group of friends that used to get together. They got married and moved here, a couple of them. They had wives and children. So I thought when my wife arrives, she will have somebody to talk to. I brought her straight from the airport to here. And we lived in that house for a little while and then my children were born. One child was born there and then we moved here to this house where the other two were born and where we still live.

At first my wife found it very hard to settle down. Life was very different to what she was used to in India. She was from a well-off family where the girls don't work. If they want a drink of water, they just have to say, and somebody brings it to them. Somebody cooks for them, and somebody cleans and washes for them. She was from that kind of family, so when she came here, she had to get used to doing everything for herself. She had to learn how to cook, clean the toilets – which was unheard of back home! Within the first year, the first child was also born. My wife used to cry a lot. She used to get very upset. She had a very rough time. Luckily, I was an excellent cook. I had to learn when I came here. I taught her a few things. Now she's better than me. If she goes away anywhere, she doesn't have to worry about me because I can look after the house and I can cook for myself.

Mrs Pramila Desai

After I finished school at 17, my father became very sick. My father was still working, even though he was ill. He was the strong one in the family and we were very close. I was the youngest in my family and unmarried, and my father said it would make him happy to see me married. So I didn't go to college because it would have been another five years of studying. My brother started looking for a husband for me. He looked for a groom in a different village. It was the community system because, if you marry in the same village, people think you are related.

My husband came from a big town with electricity, much more advanced than my village. It was just like London to me. My husband came from Nariyad. I didn't feel scared because my brother was

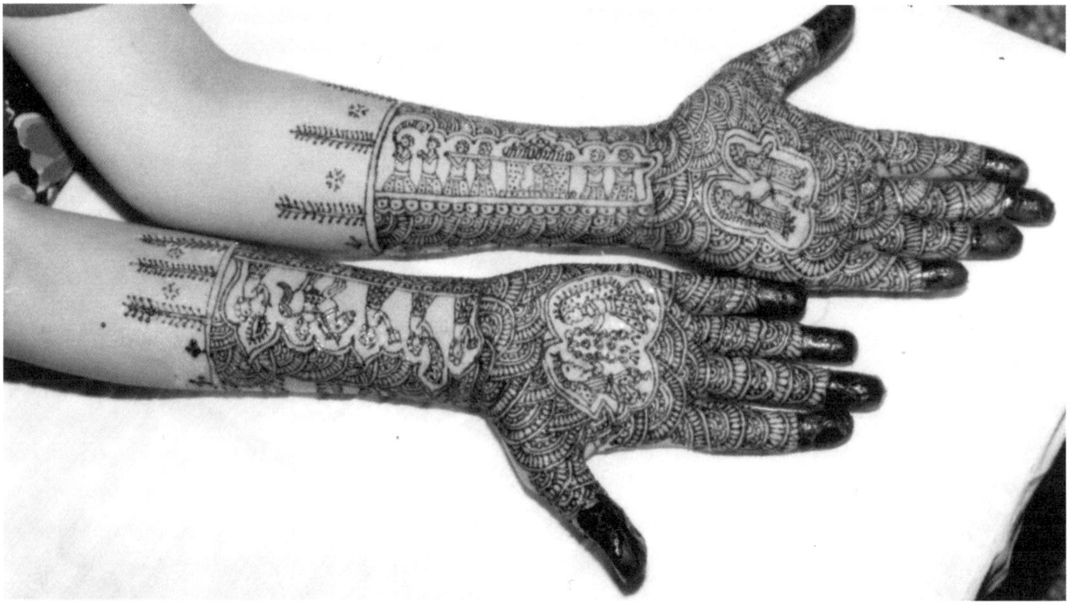

Henna is painted on to the hands and feet, staining them like a 'temporary tattoo'

married to his sister, so I didn't feel like a stranger. I remember, before I was married, I went to my husband's town for a Matric exam, because my village was very small and I couldn't take the exam there. I went to my friend's house to do the exam and he was there. My brother knew him and was keen to get me engaged to him, but I didn't know that at the time. I did tell my brother though, that if I ever wanted to get married, the boy had to be from Nariyad because it was a famous town!

When he met me, he asked me some questions about studying. I even met my future mother-in-law and she was very nice. I remember I was really dressed up, because when we went to town we made an effort. I was wearing a sari. After twelve years old you always have to wear sari. Before then, girls could wear dresses, it was the community rule! So my brother reported back to my father that he had found the right person, very educated and rich as well! We then made a contract. I met my husband I liked him. I was happy that he had a big house, much bigger than mine, and servants. I am being honest, that was my dream. Times were changing and my wedding arrangements were very different from my older sister who was arranged at 12. She didn't even see her husband for the next five years and then she saw him and went to his house, but mine was very different.

As I was the last one to get married, my brother wanted a big wedding in my village, but at the time there was death in the family. The person who had died was only 27 years old and the community forbade the wedding because of the death, we had to wait three months. Once again it was the community rules! The community rules are made by the elders in the village, and you have to accept them, whether you like it or not. Finally the wedding happened in my village, and it went on for three days.

Before the wedding day you wore special clothes. I couldn't choose my clothes. It is the custom that my mother's brother would bring the clothes. We call him 'Mama' and I have to wear what he brings. I wore a sari. It was white with a beautiful red border. I had henna on my hands one day before the wedding. My husband wore white silk 'kurtha pajama' (shirt and trousers).

On the first day of the wedding, all the relatives from outside the village arrived. We sang and danced and everyone had fun. On the second day, the ceremony took place at my house in the garden which was all decorated. My brother had a dream of drawing a map of India. He gathered some sawdust, dyed it different colours and drew a map. On the third day, my husband's side of the family arrived. They are called the 'jann.' This is the main day. The whole street was invited to the wedding. Everyone ate a wonderful feast. It was a big event. At the end of the night there was music and fireworks.

Mrs Sheila Rakhit

My fiancée's family were family friends and lived not far from us. In India the arrangements always go like that. The middleman is another family friend, who kind-of negotiates. It's just one of those things, you know, an Indian girl has to accept. It's not a legal thing, but a social and family thing. So you don't go to a completely strange family. It's a friend of a family, and it's like that. Still, I only met him about two or three weeks before we got married. So it was a big step in my life.

I am told I looked very pretty at the wedding. I wore a red sari. Red is like the white in Britain – the sign of the virginity and all that. In India, the religious marriage ceremony happened during the night time, and it was a very stormy, thundery, rainy night in the month of August, which is the rainy season back home. And I think the photos got spoiled and everything, and didn't come out. So I feel very sorry that I can't see those photographs, but I remember it well.

Courtship & Marriage Creative Activities

OLDER PEOPLE'S ACTIVITIES

Arranging the Marriage

The weddings described in this chapter often took a very long time to plan and negotiations involved both families and many other people. Can the group members remember who was involved in planning and arranging their marriage? Make a list for each person of the 'cast' involved in the whole ritual from start to finish and compare these within the group. Do not forget the match-maker, the group of advisers, the priests, the neighbours, the parents on both sides, the brothers and sisters.

A photograph of Sheila Rakhit taken to send to prospective suitors

My Wedding Day

Ask the older people to bring in wedding photos if they have them and to share the stories of their weddings. Where, who and when did they marry?

Ask members of the group to supply from memory the menu for their wedding feast. This should involve much common experience, as well as some very special features according to country and culture. Put these menus up on display so that everyone in the group can enjoy reading them and remember his or her own.

Ask people to make a list of the people who came to their wedding and any presents they received on that occasion. Have any of the group kept things dating back to their weddings? If so, can they bring them in to show to the group?

Invite members of the group to become the 'couple', 'guests', and the priest in a re-creation of one of the group's weddings, as though they are in a still photograph. This often helps people to remember who was there and what happened.

A Night to Remember, or Forget!

Wedding night stories can be very fascinating, but maybe invite people to share these with just one other person in the group first. If some people feel comfortable with reporting to the whole group (no physical details required!) this will be a most effective memory trigger and often a great source of hilarity!

Changing Times & Customs

How do members of the group feel about the marriages their families arranged for them? Were they happy to be marrying, and did they have confidence in their family's choice for them?

How many of the group have wished for similar marriages for their children and how many have been disappointed in their children's attitudes? How have members of the group come to terms with change in this matter? Do they have advice for one another?

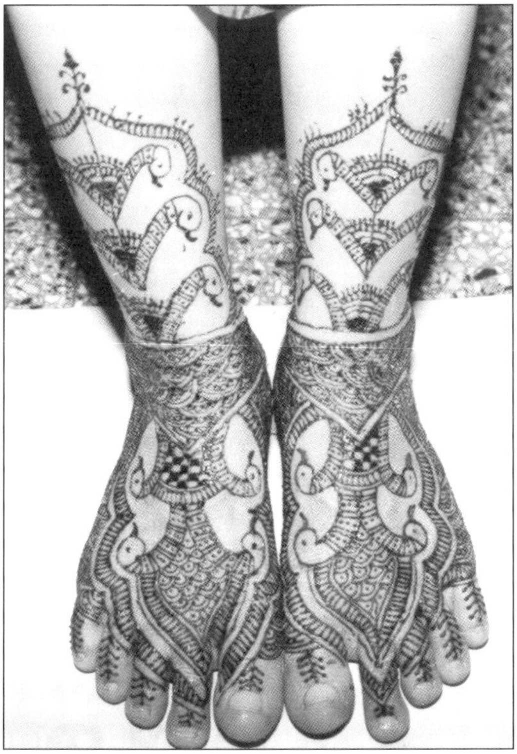

YOUNG PEOPLE'S ACTIVITIES

Arranged Marriages

It is striking how many of our story-tellers had arranged marriages. The young women often did not see their husbands before the wedding day, and certainly were not left alone with them until after the ceremony was completed. How do you think you would react to this situation? Can you see a value in the system of parents choosing a partner for their children? Bear in mind recent statistics suggesting that one in three 'love marriages' ends in divorce. Hold a debate in the classroom and argue the case for and against arranged marriage.

A Serious Business

Some of the rituals associated with marriage, especially in China, India and Africa, are extremely lengthy and complicated. Engagement and marriage could take months, or even years to arrange and complete, with many transactions on both sides. Often marriage involved the elaborate linking of both families, and many experts, advisers and matchmakers. What effect do you think this kind of ritual has on the young couple and their attitude to marriage?

The Most Important Person

Can you enter into the thoughts of a young woman who has been told that she will be married to someone from another town whom she has never met and with whom she will now go through all these rituals? Write a poem or an 'interior monologue' about your thoughts and feelings, your hopes and fears. Then do this exercise as a young man going through the same experience.

Wedding Movie

Take one of the more exciting courtship and marriage stories, like Mr Ke Wing Pang from China or Mrs Josephine Macpeppele Ja Ja from Africa, and make a storyboard out of the various stages go through. This involves making a small picture of each stage and writing the sound or speech underneath each picture.

Bringing the Past to Life

If one or two older people from different ethnic backgrounds could be encouraged to visit the classroom and talk about their memories of courtship and marriage rituals, the class could play these out under instruction from the older person. Any special songs or prayers could be learned by the class.

"It Was Different In My Day"

Many of the story-tellers have had to come to terms with great changes in the matter of courtship and marriage. Try to enter into the feelings of someone who grew up in a time of arranged marriages and has had to accept that their children and grandchildren think differently. Write a letter to an imaginary child or grandchild of yours, explaining why you are concerned for their future and wish that they would follow the traditional customs for their own good.

Chapter Four: Leaving Home

CHINESE ELDERS

Mr Ke Wing Pang

I went to Britain in 1958. My intention was to earn and save money for about three to four years and return back to Hong Kong. I am not highly educated and it was difficult to find work in Hong Kong so I came over as an economic migrant. However, I found that when I came here, I didn't make a lot of money. I went on my own to Britain and my wife stayed behind to look after the farm and the house. At that time I had one son, but later on I had a daughter and another son.

I decided to secure a job before I reached Britain. I knew it wouldn't be easy to find work once I arrived. I wrote to friends already there about work in restaurants. Eventually I got a reply that there was work and this was like having a sponsor. I didn't really have any impressions of what life in Britain would be like. All I knew was that I going to be working in restaurant kitchens. I thought if I came to Britain my weekly wage would be equivalent to two months pay in Hong Kong.

For my journey I packed clothes, a duvet, bedding, and I took some money. I didn't pack many Chinese clothes because I was told that people didn't really wear

Pang's passport picture

them so I bought western clothes. I took a mini cab to Kaitak Airport in Hong Kong. It was the first time I had flown. The flight was 72 hours long and it took over two days! I was a little bit afraid, but seven of my cousins came as well, although we didn't sit together on the plane. I sat next to an English man who was very helpful. He showed me how to eat with a knife and fork, and ordered me wine. I had never had liquor before. I couldn't understand much and I didn't realise you get free alcohol on the plane. Once all my cousins realised that I was drinking free alcohol, they all put up their hands and ordered wine as well. We changed planes about three or four times before we reached Holland and changed again because in those days there were no direct flights. I arrived at the airport and then I took a coach to Victoria.

Mrs Phuong La

My reasons for leaving my country were not straightforward. There were many upheavals before I came to Britain. I will begin from the time after I got married in China. My husband and I transferred with the cigarette company we worked for to Vietnam in 1945. We settled in a town called Hai Phong. I was pregnant at the time and found it very difficult to carry out heavy manual work in the factory, so they transferred me to a lighter packing job. The company was competing unsuccessfully with an established French cigarette factory, and in the end it moved back to China as it was not proving profitable in Vietnam.

We remained behind in Vietnam when the factory left and my husband took up a teaching job. I set up a store selling make-up and bits and pieces. But gradually more and more constraints were being placed on Chinese people. We were under pressure to change our nationality. If we didn't agree to this, then restrictions were placed on what jobs we could do. The types of jobs we couldn't do were hairdressing, police, managers and owning businesses. This forced many people out of the country because they couldn't survive on the low-paid work they were allowed to take. A friend of mine was a high-ranking police officer but, once the restrictions were put in place, he was sacked and he ended up working in a fish sauce factory. My son-in-law was also in threat of losing his job. His parents couldn't take him out of the country so, as we were deciding to leave, we smuggled him out with our daughter who was expecting a baby at that time.

Then the Vietnamese tightened their control and started deporting the Chinese back to China unless they became Vietnamese. My son and daughter didn't wait to get the official paperwork required to enter China; they just went ahead, wading through the river which separates Vietnam from China and they ended up in a refugee camp over there. My husband and I completed all the official paperwork to get back to China properly. It took three to four months to come through, but we needed it if we were to get permission to take our belongings out with us.

We left Vietnam in 1978. We got the train to China and stayed in a refugee camp for a few months. We met up with my son there and decided to despatch him to Hong Kong. Some people who were leaving took him with them when they were going to Hong Kong and, once he arrived safely, he wrote to me to let me know.

In the refugee camp the government gave us 15 Yuan, but this wasn't enough to live on. The UN gave us food packets for one month and then you had to find your own food and work. My husband went

Mrs La became one of the boat people

and cooked in the camp. Luckily, I found a factory outside the camp, which employed people up to the age of 40. I was 50, but I looked younger and I was lucky. I went to one of the ladies who was working in the factory and said, "Please give me work there. I will have nothing to do here in the camp and I have a family to feed." They asked me in the factory if I was Vietnamese. I said, "I am Chinese and I just went to Vietnam for work." In the end they gave me work. The camp was full of people who had fled from Vietnam. Even though I was born in China, they didn't grant me residency there. I waited to hear from my son. He had to appeal on our behalf once he got to Hong Kong. Eventually we received the letter saying we could come to Hong Kong. So my husband, my youngest daughter and I decided to leave the camp. My other daughter who was married remained behind with her husband. We travelled to Canton, then on to Pak Hoi.

I was 58 when I went to Hong Kong. We sailed there in a small fishing boat from Pak Hoi. Sadly, all my documents got wet, my marriage papers and photographs. I didn't have much in the way of belongings. Most of it was stolen when I was in Vietnam. So I was very upset when all that remained had also been destroyed on the fishing boat, which was very unstable. It was a huge risk going by boat; there were so many people. But we were prepared to risk our lives. We just wanted to make sure our son was safe and to join him. After midnight, in the darkness, we were transferred to a big fishing boat and then, in the morning, we were moved to a big trawler. We spent two nights and one day on the trawler. Then about three in the morning, we changed to the little boats again because the big trawler was not allowed to go any further. It was against the law for the big boats to sail into Hong Kong, so the little boats were pulled to a certain point by the big boat, and it then turned back towards China. We arrived in Hong Kong at seven in the morning and a police boat came out. We pulled out a white flag asking for help. At eight in the morning, two strong men were employed to row the boats. The police came to the little boats and took down our details. They gave us hot water and biscuits and allowed us to come ashore.

Mrs Ah Poh Luong

We came to Britain because the Vietnamese authorities deported us. The Vietnamese

Mrs Loung's green ID book, which the Vietnamese authorities wanted to change

authorities wanted me to give up my Chinese nationality and assume Vietnamese nationality. I had retained my Chinese identity even though I was born in Vietnam because both my parents were Chinese. They had kept their Chinese identity after leaving China because of the Japanese Occupation. I had a green ID book which the Vietnamese wanted me to change. The Vietnamese authorities tried to reclaim my book and issue me with another one. This was happening on every street corner, but my husband and I refused. Anyone who refused had to leave; it did not matter who or where you were. Even my parents and the rest of my family left.

The Vietnamese government wanted to conscript Chinese men into their army by changing their nationality to Vietnamese, but we didn't want that. Very few Chinese changed their identity because no one wanted their husbands and sons to be conscripted. We went to the Chinese Embassy and they negotiated with the Vietnamese government. It was agreed that those who refused to sign and change their nationalities would be allowed to return to China. Once this was agreed, China asked Vietnam to open the dividing bridge to allow people back into China. We crossed the bridge and there were Chinese welcoming us back.

In China, we stayed in a refugee camp for a few weeks and then we left for Hong Kong by boat. Boats were arranged to take people to Hong Kong but you had to pay to cross and we did not have enough money. We went in separate directions because we could not pay to go all together. We simply followed wherever others were going and, with the help of friends and relatives, we were all able to leave China. My husband, sons, daughters and daughters-in-law went across to Hong Kong. I followed with my younger son and daughter-in-law on a friend's boat and we ended up in Macao.

When my husband reached Hong

Kong, he registered to settle either in England or Canada, but I was stuck in Macao, and people from Macao were encouraged to go to America. My son wrote to me urging me not to got to America, otherwise we would be separated. After three weeks in Hong Kong, my son managed to get to England. It was a difficult time. I was living in the camp and was given $8 a day. I was being pressured to go to America and I complained and asked them, "Why would you send me to America when my husband is still over here in Hong Kong and my son is in England?" When I went and complained, I asked them what sort of paperwork they needed and I then told my son to organise it all. So finally, after two years, I was reunited with my family.

Mrs Makfung San

In May 1978, all the Chinese people in Vietnam, had to leave the country. They weren't given any time or any warning. From what I remember, if you were Chinese, people would just make a more difficult life for you, even your neighbours. Gradually, they showed they didn't like you, and they tried to kick you out. And especially when you're trading and you've got your own shop, I tried doing my own business. I would do anything that could get money, anything! Buying and selling, buying and selling.

But the police kept on coming round, and you have to give them money all the time. So it made life very difficult. And the people keep on asking, "When are you going back to your own country?". And in the place where we lived, they had two Chinese schools in the city, but they shut them down. They wouldn't take any Chinese pupils.

I was already a grandmother. My husband had already died. At this time of life, you don't expect big changes and big moves. Everything seemed so settled. Well, I sold everything, all the furniture. Everything was sold! I can't remember how much I took with me. A lot of money though. I remember giving money to my children, and my grandsons. The whole family left together, even though the children didn't want to come. People forced you because you would find nothing to eat there, and you would die.

From Tong Tang we took a coach to Pakhoi, a harbour town in China. We travelled by coach for three days and three nights, a non-stop drive, with all the children and grandchildren. It was much better for us there than in Vietnam. And from Pakhoi you could sail in a boat to Hong Kong. In Bachai, they had an organisation and they knew which people had run from Vietnam and needed to get away. They would come and ask you if you wanted to leave in their boats. We got a very small boat to Hong Kong, with just 36 people on it, and we had to pay the captain. We left in secret under cover of night.

We were at sea for roughly twenty days, but some sailings took a month or more. It depended how fast they were able to sail. The children were very sick, but they survived. They just ate rice. People were vomiting and very ill. All my old photographs were lost in the sea during the journey.

When we got to Hong Kong we had to make a lot of noise and sound to draw attention to ourselves, and then immigration services would come and pick us up. And they took us to a place called Hat Chong. That's a place where they would take you, like a big hall to register, and you would temporarily live there.

You had to get on the coach, or bus, to go in there, You had to live there for a few days before going into the camp, because they needed to check up where you had come from, and whether you are qualified to stay in Hong Kong. And then we were registered, and a few days later you could go to the camp. There were thousands of people in the camp, all waiting to leave Hong Kong to go to different countries, and see which countries would accept us.

We had food, drink, everything. I didn't have to worry about anything! I came by air to England, my first time in an aeroplane. When I arrived in England, there were newspaper people coming to take pictures. I was in the newspaper. When I arrived in England, I was very happy. I felt like a film star! I wondered why everyone came to watch me arrive!

Mrs Suk Tsang Tang

We decided to leave Vietnam in 1981 to escape the Communists. A lot of Chinese people were trying to leave at this point. The problem was between Chinese and Vietnamese people from the end of 1977 onwards. The Vietnamese were more allied to the Soviet Union. So the Chinese minority in Vietnam were threatened by that, by the conflict between China and Vietnam. They became very unpopular in Vietnam, and the Vietnamese said, "Go! We don't want Chinese people here. This is not your country. Go back to your own".

My husband was ill at that point. In 1977, my son and I left my husband and the other children and ran to a place in the mountains. We stayed there for six months. Then we went to a place near the sea, but there was terrible flooding in that area and so we prepared to go home to Saigon again. But on our journey back, halfway there, we stayed with an aunt who gave us some money, so I went with my son to help him get on to a boat. It took him a long time to get here and settle in the UK.

Eventually I too came over with one of my daughters. My son was living in King's Cross. He had found work in the dim sum department of the airport caterers working for Japanese Airlines. He met his wife over here, a Chinese Vietnamese girl. A very nice girl. I met her when I came over here. They had got married here and had children – two sons.

Mrs Belmont Williams

I left Freetown for England in 1953. I had been awarded a full scholarship to study medicine. I travelled by sea in the Apapa mail vessel. At that time three mail ships went between Freetown and Liverpool and the journey took nine days with one stop at Las Palmas in the Canary Islands. I was lucky to have travelled with my father who was coming to meet my mother. My mother was then the Commissioner of the Sierra Leone Girl Guides Association and had come to England leading six Girl Guides to attend the Coronation of Queen Elizabeth in 1953. My brother was already at Queens University in Belfast, so an aunt of ours moved into our home in Sierra Leone to take care of my three sisters and other children.

I was very sorry to be leaving my sisters, but at the same time I was very excited about going to England. Several other students travelled with me on that boat. They were also coming to England to study for various degrees and qualifications at different colleges and universities in England, Scotland, Wales and Northern Ireland. We were on full scholarships so we all travelled first class on the boat. I shared the cabin with another student who was going to study for a Bachelor of Science Degree. We thoroughly enjoyed the trip. All the passengers dressed up for the evening meal and there were functions and activities at night, including a formal dinner and dance on the last night.

I did not do much in the way of preparations for leaving home. Both my parents had been to England several times before and advised me on what it would be like. My father also used to get us the children's English newspapers and, as both the principal and vice-principal of the secondary school I attended were of British nationality, I knew quite a lot about England. However it was the first time I was leaving home.

Mrs Josephine Macpeppele Ja Ja

My husband wanted to carry on his studying and that was the reason we had to come to England. He left for London first. He came by ship and I saw him off from Port Apapa. I don't remember now why we didn't go together, but I know that when I came over here, I travelled alone. I came by plane and was feeling happy because I was going to see my husband. Some other people were so scared that they couldn't eat their food on the plane, but I ate mine. When we were approaching Britain, they told us that we had to go to the bathroom and have a wash. When we got off the plane it was really cold; that was my first feeling. It was October and it was windy, but as we were approaching the sunlight, it was really beautiful. My husband met me at the airport with extra coats and cardigans. I had to wear two cardigans with a big top coat. My mother brought the children over to England a bit later on.

Mr Ade Aderogba

I was already a chartered secretary before I left Nigeria. I remember my boss, the bursar of the University of Ibadan, Mr Alpott, called me in when I resigned, and said, "My boy, why do you want to go to England? What is the need? You've got 'O' Levels, 'A' Levels, you are an ACIS, you could just wait for promotion; just carry on here." And I said, "No, all my friends are going. If only for the adventure, I will go." I wasn't quite sure what I wanted to do when I got to England, but I knew I wanted to gain more work experience. I never thought of myself as a migrant to the UK. I was a student, and that is what it said on my passport and my visa.

In May 1965, I bought a ticket from Lagos to Liverpool for £82. The company was called Elder Dempster Lines, one of the main shipping lines between Liverpool and West Africa. They took manufactured engineering goods to West Africa and brought back cargo such as cocoa, palm oil and timber. It was a cargo ship which allowed ten or fifteen passengers, but you had to book well in advance. So I told my mum, and she echoed the same words as my boss, "What do you want to go to England for? I was trying to save the money to buy you a car". But I said, "Mum, I've got to travel", she replied, "All right then!"

Leaving home was an emotional thing. I did not travel alone. My cousin, Olaweirai Babalola, a bit older than me, also worked for the University of Ibadan in the Geology department, when I was in Finance, and we resigned at the same time. Our brothers came to see us off and stood on the harbour wall waving while we boarded this cargo boat. The ship took two weeks to cross from Lagos to Liverpool. As it was a cargo boat, it stopped in Ghana to pick up cocoa, and then in Sierra Leone. The captain said, "Now ladies and gentlemen,

2

DESCRIPTION *SIGNALEMENT*

Bearer *Titulaire* | Wife *Femme*

Profession / *Profession*: STUDENT

Place and date of birth / *Lieu et date de naissance*: OSHOGBO 21·7·1942.

Country of Residence / *Pays de Résidence*: NIGERIA

Height / *Taille*: 5 ft. 11 ins. | ft. in.

Colour of eyes / *Couleur des yeux*: BROWN

Colour of hair / *Couleur des cheveux*: BLACK.

Special peculiarities / *Signes particuliers*

CHILDREN *ENFANTS*

Name *Nom* | Date of birth *Date de naissance* | Sex *Sexe*

CANCELLED

Usual signature of bearer / *Signature du titulaire*

Usual signature of wife / *Signature de sa femme*

3

Bearer *Titulaire*

Wife *Femme*

(PHOTO)

The passport Ade used as he departed from Africa to study in Britain in 1965

fellow passengers, you can go offshore for two days, and then come back because we are loading". So I was given a pass and off I went to Freetown – I visited Sierra Leone. I also stopped off at Las Palmas in the Canaries; they were beautiful islands. It felt like I had a free holiday.

I landed at Liverpool Docks in June 1965. The immigration officer was very courteous and acknowledged that I had a student visa and good qualifications. Many migrants who came from Nigeria had work permits because they were coming over as electrical engineers, or as nurses who came here to save lives. People tend to forget that not all black people came here as beggars and illegal immigrants. It is something I feel white people should be aware of today, and to remember that the British sent double-decker buses to Jamaica and trained people as bus conductors because they were needed in the 'mother country' in the years after the war.

Mr Anthony Maduagwu

I left home in 1964, and came over here to London and I am still here. My colleagues at work introduced me to the idea. We had two white people from England, who were working with us, and one of them said to me, "Why not go to England to further your education?" Well, I organised a visa for myself, but at this time I had been made a foreman in charge of technical drawing and I wasn't sure I wanted to come. You know my visa expired three times, and had to be renewed, so the visa people at the Embassy said to me that if this one expired they wouldn't give me another. When I came to London, it had only three days left to run. It was an employment visa, and I got a school admission letter for studying as well.

My Mum wasn't happy at all, especially me being the first-born son. She reckoned I was going to die, because I might not be able to feed myself as I never did any cooking at home. I said to her, "Mum, I will not die." Anyway, she said "yes", because she knew I could eat anything to survive so that is why she allowed me.

When I was coming, I just had a small suitcase of clothes and an address to come to. I paid the fare and sent some money to England through the bank so that when I arrived here I'd just have to collect it and there would be no big fuss about it. I thought it was the land of gold and silver, but when I came here, I found out that when I applied for work, some people said "Go back home, you nigger".

Mr James Adebayo Adesina

In 1960, when I was about twenty-six, I decided to come to Great Britain to study. I saved hard and I put in an application for a passport. We were not yet a free country – we were still under a colonial power – so in those days it was still a British colonial passport with a hard cover, the only difference being that they put the word 'Nigeria' on it. Luckily, I knew somebody who knew somebody who assisted me and I got my passport; in fact I've still got it today.

I started going to training provided by the British Council because they wanted to educate us about what we would find in Britain, what our restrictions would be, what we should do. So, even though many of us had been using a fork and knife for twenty years, they taught us, saying, "You are going to hold your fork like this, and you are going to hold your spoon like this." They also showed us how to put on a bowler hat, how to roll your umbrella. When you are given something you say, "Thank you", when you want something say, "Excuse me". All sorts of good things, but I think they overstated it!

I eventually paid for my flight, which, at that time was a lot of money. I think it was about £32. I didn't fly on my own. I was with all my friends, the ones that I worked with and the ones who went to the same school. We all decided to come about the same time, and luckily, I think about forty or fifty of us travelled on the same day. I prayed that plane should not crash! It took two days to make the flight because we stopped in Libya. It was the first time I'd been on a plane and I had packed lots of suits but I still brought some native clothes and native materials, should they be needed, and some ingredients for cooking: pepper, melon, seeds which could be turned into soup.

I had certain impressions of Britain. I didn't expect to see any poor Englishmen. I thought they would all be rich, like the ones I had seen in my native land, because in Nigeria they all lived like emperors. They had a cook, a steward, a gardener, driver and cleaner, so I expected that some would be of that level.

When I flew into Heathrow airport on the second day of my journey, and I saw the country, it seemed grey and grim and not as prosperous as the one I had left behind. Back home, we like to play a lot of outdoor activities, and shout and make a lot of noise, and this whole country looked cold like a graveyard. At first I said, "Are there any living people in this country, or only dead people living here?" When a Nigerian or Yoruban man is passing, we greet each other with a shout!

Mrs Mako Herabe

I came to Britain because my daughter was here and I my husband had passed away. She had fled to England because of the civil war in Somalia, and was applying for a family reunion permit to bring me and her children over. All my family had disappeared. I didn't know where they were. I was looking after my grand-daughter and grandson. We had to leave Mogadishu because it was unsafe. I was very lonely and wanted to join my daughter. I was finally accepted because my daughter was recognised as having full refugee status. I was very sad about leaving my home, but it was something I could not avoid. I wanted to live in Somalia and I want to die in Somalia but I had to leave for my own and my grandchildren's safety, and so I could be with my daughter. Somalia was unsafe because of president Mohammed Siad Barre and his dictatorship. Initially he was building the country and helping people, but over the last 20 years he had brought his family into power, controlled, separated and isolated people. So the people started to rise against him. Instead of protecting all the country, there was rivalry and civil war, looting and killing. No-one was safe.

When we fled Somalia, we had left everything behind. I didn't make any preparations. A lorry took us from Mogadishu to Ethiopia. The journey lasted three days and three nights. When I got to Addis Ababa I waited to hear from my daughter who was making all the arrangements for me to join her. I couldn't even imagine where I was going. I just wanted to reunite with my daughter. Addis Ababa was used as a transit place for Somalians who were waiting for their families to sort out their reunions. We rented a house and my daughter communicated with me and sent me money. This transit place had a real community spirit where everyone helped each other. There were many people in the same position as me with families scattered all over Europe, Canada and America. I had to wait a whole year until I was reunited with my daughter. I was very happy and looking forward to taking my grandchildren somewhere safe with no looting or killing.

CARIBBEAN ELDERS

Mrs Irma Reid

I had always wanted to be a nurse and I wanted to go to England to train. My father said, "Why don't you train in Trinidad?" I replied that I could train in Trinidad, but there was a five year waiting list, so he gave in and agreed that I could come. However, my dad wasn't keen for me to go on my own. My sister Christiana had always wanted to go to a secretarial college and qualified in shorthand, typing and book-keeping, but in the end she decided to come over with me. I always had a fondness for England, having read lots of literature, like Thomas Hardy and Shakespeare. I loved English and I loved literature! My impression of England was rosy, not like what I found when I first arrived. I imagined it to be like a traditional Christmas card, with houses covered in snow like a real fairy tale!

I wrote an application form to the Matron at Grove Park Hospital in south London and she replied and agreed for both of us to come over. I was very excited and looking forward to going, but I was also dreading it because we were a very close family and had never been separated.

I decided to make clothes for Christiana and myself. I was fairly good at sewing and picked up tips from my mum. I went and purchased some lovely material and made two coats. Mine was black and

Irma's mother, who taught her to sew

silver, with a fur collar and a thick lining to keep me warm. Christiana's was a brown and black material, also very warm.

My older brother, who had joined the police force gave us the equivalent of 20 pounds each as spending money, which was quite a lot at that time. My father arranged the fare for the cruise ship. We were going to be sailing on the 'Oriana'. I rang up the agent and asked how much it would cost. It was much cheaper than a flight which at that time was $735 and the boat fare was $527.

As our departure came closer, I went shopping and bought things for the trip, everyone was really helpful. My friends requested a song to be played on the radio for me. I think it was "I am leaving on a jet plane." I remember the lady on the radio station saying, " You know this is for Irma Reid and Christiana who are going to England to study nursing," and she said, "Oh Irma Reid, that is a nice name." Our pictures were even in the local paper. I remember going through Mum's papers after she died and found that she had kept that press-cutting all this time. I made a special outfit for the journey. It was the brightest yellow material, we used to wear 'fat pants' which were like culottes, very wide, and a multi-coloured top.

I was 24 and Christiana was 20 when we left. We travelled by boat.The departure was very emotional. The worst part about it was that the harbour wasn't deep enough for large ships to come in, so we had to go out in small boats and only two people were allowed to come on the boat with us. So we had to leave my mum and some of my brothers and sisters behind. It was horrendous and you know, because we are a very close family, it made me feel horrible. We shared a cabin with two other Trinidadian girls.

The journey took 11 days, which was quick in those days; most of my friends who went by boat said it took them 23 days. There weren't that many black people on the ship but we didn't experience any racism, and everybody talked to us. The cabin staff were mainly Indian and they couldn't speak any English, but we used to try and talk to them. We thought everybody spoke English. There was one particular Indian chap who was very fond of me and when I went to have a shower in the morning, and return to my room there were flowers on the bed or a parcel of bread, cakes or biscuits. I was very naïve in those days and I was very embarrassed.

We were even invited to the captain's cocktail party. Christiana and I went with two other girls. We found the food on the boat a bit bland so the Indian staff used to leave mangoes, tabasco sauce, and pickles for us and this made the food spicy and more pleasant. On our journey we saw different islands such as Barbados, St Thomas, the Virgin Islands and when we reached Europe, we stopped at Lisbon. Finally, we docked at Southampton and took the train to Waterloo.

Mr Michael Roper

I came to Britain from Jamaica in 1951. My aunt was living in England and she invited me over to help her to look after her house. She said, "Come on Michael, come to England". I was 20 years old and my mother didn't know I had gone out and purchased a ticket. Eventually I told her. I also had to sort out my passport, and reserve a cabin on the boat. I was going to sail on a big cruise ship and I think it was Italian. I had a big farewell party before I left and everyone was dancing. I was excited and saw my journey as an adventure. I danced with my girlfriend and said goodbye to her and my baby boy.

Everyone was so excited that I didn't have time to think about leaving home. Friends of mine got a collection going. I think they raised about £80 and that was a complete surprise. I was very drunk when I boarded the ship and, when I saw my cabin, I was really shocked that it was so basic. I said, "What kind of cabin this? I paid for a room and this room looks like a cell, I am not paying for this!" But I was getting what I paid for. An Italian lady felt sorry for me and offered me a drink, and we danced to the Italian music. Every night was a party. I also ate swordfish and I remember throwing up. I was on the boat for 14 days. We were heading for Dover and I was looking forward to seeing those white cliffs.

Mrs Gladys Smith

I lost my husband in 1959. He died suddenly and I decided to leave the island of Aruba where we had been living and return to St Vincent where I grew up. I tried to build my own house on St Vincent, but I couldn't settle. For a few months I worked for a solicitor and then I worked in a bank. After building this house, I wanted to

much beyond the village. I had never been on a train. I was then dropped at the airport. I had never been on a plane either. I was really scared. I had seen planes fly but I had never seen them on the ground. I travelled during the night; my plane was one hour late. We were told that it had broken down so I was waiting, and that didn't help my nerves. I travelled on my own on the plane. I was really scared, a young 20 year old going on a plane. I couldn't even eat the food. I was feeling really sick, but luckily I had brought some chapattis from home. The people on the plane were mostly English. There was one lady who spoke Hindi, so I spoke a bit with her. I felt a little bit more comfortable after that.

Mrs Sheila Rakhit

At the time I came here, I'd just got married. A date had to be selected as an auspicious one, for us to come here. And this was fixed by our parents. I am a Hindu and usually we consult a holy book; it's like a calendar but with much more detail of the auspicious times – good times, and bad times and that.

I knew when I married that I would have to accompany my husband to England. I knew that I would have to adjust and accommodate my life to his. And for me to come to this country was a big adventure, to follow my husband to come here. I remember vividly the day I said

goodbye to my parents. I cried really loudly! When I think of it, I feel very silly. But it wasn't silly. I needed to cry, you know, because I was the oldest of four children. I was only twenty-three, and it was very painful for me to leave my brothers and sisters, and mum and dad and all that. Leaving everybody behind and coming here was a very big thing for me.

Leaving Home Creative Activities

OLDER PEOPLE'S ACTIVITIES

Packing For the Journey

Do you remember packing for your departure? Who helped you or did you prepare alone? Were there special mementos you felt you must bring with you to remind you of home? Make a list of all the items each person brought with them. This will help others to remember their own and there will probably be many things in common.

One Thing I've Still Got

Do you still have any of these items which you brought with you? Maybe you could bring them in to show the group and make a small exhibition together of things which have survived the ups and downs of life in England.

What I Looked Like

Did you buy any special clothes for your journey, or have them made up for you before leaving? Who helped with this? Do you have a photo of yourself before your departure, dressed for the journey? If not, draw a picture to show what you were wearing and carrying.

How I Felt

What were your feelings on departure? Were you scared, excited, sad, optimistic, or a mixture of all these and other feelings? Did you tell anyone how you felt when you were leaving?

"Last Glimpse Photo of Home"

If you could take a 'mental photograph' of your last sight of your native land as you stepped on the boat or plane, what would the photo contain? Were there friends and family members to wave you off? Draw an image on paper of what would have been your 'last glimpse photo of home' if one had been taken.

Farewell Photo

Alternatively, arrange other people in the group as if they were the family you were leaving behind. Tell them who they are representing and what your memories are of the people concerned. If you remember the kind of things they said, give each person a phrase associated with the person they are representing.

Destination Unknown

What image did you have of the Britain you were coming to? Had you seen photos or films beforehand? Did you have an idea of what would happen when you arrived?

Have Passport, Will Travel

Do you still have your original passport? What do you feel when you look at the picture of the young you, setting out on this adventure?

Pramila's farewell photo to her husband

My Journey
Can you chart your journey from your home country to England? Using a ribbon or string, pin your route on to a map which includes the important places you stopped at or passed through. Share your journey with others in the group and put the journeys you have mapped around the walls of the room. Take time to imagine one another's journeys, to find common stopping places and to identify similar experiences.

Coming Back Home Soon?
So many people came to England expecting to stay just a few years, save money and go home to settle. What were the factors which kept you here and prevented you from returning home with money after a few years? Were they economic factors, such as the difficulty in finding work which was well paid? Or was it the higher cost of living? Or was it emotional attachments and new relationships which made you decide to stay?

If I Had My Life Over Again
Do you feel it has worked out as you thought it would at that point? If you had your life over again, would you make the same decision to leave your home country? Compare your answer and your reasons with others in the group.

YOUNG PEOPLE'S ACTIVITIES

Journey Into The Unknown
Imagine packing for a minimum five-year stay in an unknown country. What would you definitely take with you to remind you of home? What would you have to leave behind?

Farewells
How would you prepare for such a big move? Who would you need to say a special goodbye to?

Do You Have to Go?
How do you think the rest of your family would react if you decided to emigrate? What reasons might they produce to try to

prevent you from leaving? Play out a scene between a mother and son or daughter in which the parent tries to persuade the young person to stay at home. Use Ade's or Anthony's story to help you.

Big Decisions

Imagine you are considering leaving home to try life in a distant country. Divide a page down the middle and write out the pros and cons of leaving or staying. Go through them with someone else and try to decide what to do.

Window On the World

What ways do we now have of finding out about the places we are travelling to in advance? How many of these methods would have been available to the older people telling their stories in this chapter?

Everything is Different Here

So many things started to feel different for our story-tellers, even on the journey over. Consider Mr Pang having to learn how to eat with a knife and fork and having alcohol for the first time in the plane. Imagine if it was the other way round and you were flying to China to live and had to learn to eat with chop sticks, as no knives or forks would be provided. Write a postcard home to tell the family how you managed, or didn't, and draw a picture for them of your struggle with the chopsticks.

Different Journeys, Different Reasons

Choose a story in this chapter and decide if the story-teller is a refugee (someone fleeing a state of danger) or an economic migrant (someone seeking work and a better standard of living). How do you think their attitude to their journey would be affected by their reasons for leaving?

A Long, Hard Slog

Notice how indirect were the journeys of some of the story-tellers by tracing their route on a map. Some took years of travelling, often escaping from danger, before they were reunited with their families. They often had to raise large amounts of money before they could travel the next leg of their journey and much of the journeying was dangerous.

Lost at Sea

Look at Mrs La and Mrs Luong's stories. Write a diary entry for two or three days of their journey as though you were one of these women. You could include having to take the difficult decision to separate from other family members, the danger of crossing seas in tiny boats, losing important photos and certificates overboard which you had carefully preserved over many years.

Together After So Long

Many of the women in these stories had been apart from their husbands for some time, as the menfolk often came to Britain

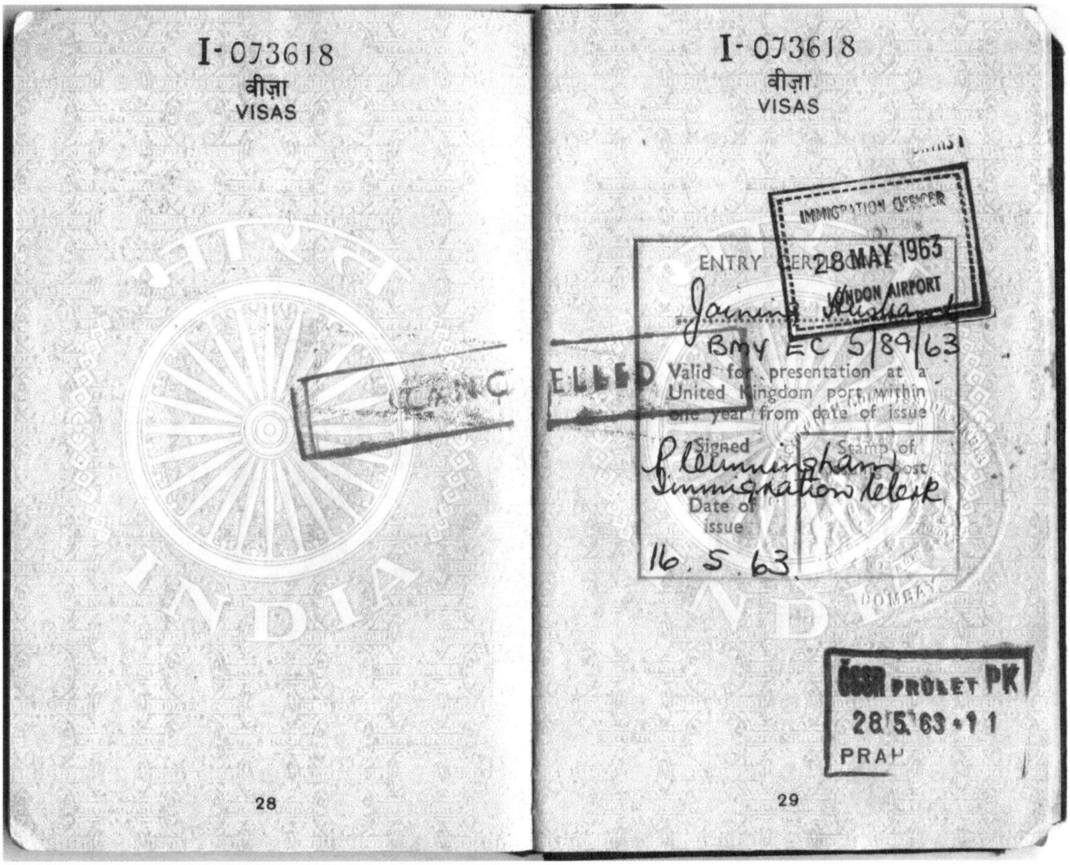

well before the rest of their families. How do you think these husbands and wives must have felt about seeing their partners after such a long separation? Remember that some of the women had not been long married in their home countries before their husbands had left for Britain.

Write an 'interior monologue' from the point of view of a young man or woman preparing to meet their partner after a long separation. What worries would be surfacing? And what hopes?

Mapping the Journey

Choose a story from this chapter and make a map to show the journey of the story-teller. Some people flew, but their journeys were often long and indirect. Many people sailed and stopped off on the way. Compare the journey you have marked out with others in the group. If there are older people willing to come to the classroom and share their journey story with the class, this marking out of routes is a good joint activity for young and old.

Chapter Five: Settling in Britain

CHINESE ELDERS

Mr Ke Wing Pang

When I arrived in London in 1962, I lived in Earl's Court. There were four of us living in one room. It was £5 for four people – £1 per person, plus £1 for the room – so £1 and 5 shillings each. There was a gas ring in the room, so I could cook soft noodles and vegetables. The people living in my room were all from Hong Kong. All I remember thinking at the time was how difficult life would be here.

My first job was in an Italian restaurant in Knightsbridge. I worked in the kitchen washing dishes. I was paid £8 a week. Ten shillings went towards National Insurance stamps. I worked on Sunday as well, but was paid £3 for that. When they told me I would be taxed £1 for working a 12-hour shift, I refused to work, as it would not be worth my while, so they didn't deduct any tax from me in the end. On the whole they were good to me. I was only working in the evening. I'd start at about 6 o'clock. I got a chance to eat Italian food like spaghetti bolognaise. During the day I went shopping, cooked lunch, nothing much really. I sometimes I took my cousins to Soho and then it was time to go to work. I don't think the Chinese were treated very well. Sometimes on the underground, if you were sitting down, English people would tell you to get up! I saw Chinese people being pulled out of their seats!

Mr Pang's wife and family

I used keep in touch with home by visiting the post office on Trafalgar Square and using the telephone service they had set up there. What happened there was you gave the number to the guy and paid for the call. You waited in the queue and, when there was a telephone free, the man would dial the number for you, and you could speak. On the whole I didn't feel lonely when I was working, but when I was alone outside working hours I did, especially when I was not feeling well. I was sending money home every month, but when the Post Office went on strike I couldn't send money for three months.

I saved enough for my fare and returned back to Hong Kong in 1966. I only paid £45 for my flight to Hong Kong. It was cheap because it was a first-come first-served stand-by arrangement. You had to wait until the plane was nearly full up with people who had booked, then you could go in a spare seat. I went for about a month for a holiday and to see my family. I was really excited and happy to see my family, my wife and son. My wife thought I had changed; I was wearing Western clothes, she was in traditional Chinese clothes. She found me a little paler and plumper! I didn't feel that different, only I found the climate a bit hot.

After a month in Hong Kong I returned to London and worked in Hampstead as a waiter in a Chinese restaurant. I lived above it. Then in 1975 my wife came over to bring our son. He was about 14. He came for education because the schooling is better here and it is free. We all stayed in the one room I rented in Acton for £7 a week.

I was working in Bayswater. I'd got a job in a Chinese restaurant working in the kitchen cutting and cleaning. I was not a trained chef and I found it very hard, but I was earning much better money, about £40 a week.

Before she left Hong Kong, my wife had given birth to our baby girl but we left her behind with her grandmother because my wife was only staying a few weeks at this point before returning to Hong Kong.

Mr Pang working in a restaurant

After she left, it was just me and my son. He settled and went to a local school. Then in 1977, my wife finally came to settle, bringing my daughter and my other son over with her. My kids liked it here. They found it easier to adjust than we did.

Initially my wife had been reluctant to come because she couldn't speak English, she couldn't read and she didn't know how to get around. However, after a week or so, she got a job washing up in the Chinese restaurant in Bayswater near the underground station and she was able to talk to other Chinese people and find her way around. Later on we moved into a bigger room, but there were still five of us living in one room and we had to share a kitchen with others. To pass the time we all used to go shopping in Chinatown, but not to the cinema as we couldn't understand the language. It was hard to maintain culture and rituals as my children were learning about English traditions rather than Chinese traditions.

Eventually we were able to save up some money and start our own takeaway business. My wife and I ran the takeaway and one of my sons who was nearly 17 helped us. I had to stop work for a while after a year because I got asthma so I couldn't work in the kitchen. I sold the lease to somebody else, and with the money I bought a house for my family in Harlow in Essex.

Mrs Phuong La

In 1981, all the paperwork was finally in order and we could travel from Hong Kong to England. We were all accepted, but my younger daughter did not come over. She had got married in Hong Kong, so she decided to stay behind with her husband. When we arrived in London, my husband, my son and I were put on a small plane to Leeds where we stayed in a refugee camp. Everyone had warned me that the camps in Britain were not very good, that they were poorly equipped and that you had to queue for food. I also heard rumours that there would be no rice, and I would have to eat mashed potatoes. In fact, the camp was good. It used to be a hospital but, because it had closed down, they used it as a temporary refugee camp. We stayed in that camp for three months and we soon got used to living there. We got unemployment benefit because the old and the young who came over had difficulties getting jobs. At the camp we had regular visits from an English teacher who taught us the language.

The Council gave us a choice of three houses in Leeds. We were not allowed to go to London unless we had relatives living there, so we settled in Leeds for the next two years. My son was doing well at school and wanted to go for higher education, but he was turned down for a course in Leeds. He then applied for a place on a better course in Newcastle, which included learning English to a higher level, and he was accepted. Around this time, the council had to renovate our house in Leeds because it was old and cold and they were putting in central heating. We had to move out while the renovations were done. The teacher from the camp suggested we talk to the council about moving to Newcastle and they agreed so we were given a council house up there. My son, now 22, studied in Newcastle to become an interpreter for Chinese and Vietnamese clubs. I also worked as an interpreter for one year. Then my son went back to China to get married. On his return, he moved to London and he found work as a jeweller. Then I also applied to go to London and this was allowed now that my son was there.

Mrs Ah Poh Luong

I was about 59 when I arrived in Britain. The Government sent people to collect refugees from the airport and take us to a camp. I don't remember where it was. Then my husband and son came to pick me up. My husband had found a nice house where we could all live together: my husband, son and my daughter-in-law. Early on, I found it a little bit hard because I didn't know the language. I enjoyed going to the markets, although they were not like the markets back home. When my son first moved out from the family home to be a student, he didn't live too far away, but people were worried about us, thinking we were lonely. We even got a visit from an English priest to see if we were all right. By then, my husband and I were retired and where we lived, there wasn't a large Chinese community, but we did have a few friends and we passed the time going out with them. We then made a request to move to London, and after two years we were able to come to London to settle.

We all preferred living in London. I didn't really get to know people from other communities, but London was a really mixed society and we felt more at home here. And there was a much larger Chinese community here. We were living in a flat in Greenwich, near the Cutty Sark ship. I stayed there for many years until I moved to a sheltered housing unit for Chinese elders called Kenneth Lee House.

Mrs Makfung San

They welcomed me and took my family to a camp. I can't remember which part of England it was. And the camp was a very nice, comfortable place. I was in the camp for three months and then I was brought to see a property in Deptford. If I liked it, I could go back and pick up all my stuff, but if I didn't like it I could go back and stay in the camp for longer. But I liked it, so I came to live here in Deptford. My house is very near this centre, off Evelyn Street, Ross Street. The whole family lived together there.

By the time I arrived here, I was quite old, so I didn't have to do any work. But the children, when they first arrived here, were on Income Support. But now all the sons have got their own jobs. The grandchildren still go to school and university. My grandchildren all speak English, but with me, they speak Cantonese. I speak my own Chinese dialect – *Leung San*. So I am very happy that I am here. This is the place that I want to be. I love it here.

Mrs Belmont Williams

The boat docked at Liverpool and we travelled by train to London, Euston. My mother, some friends and representatives of the British Council met us at the station. I went to stay with my parents in a flat in Tooting Bec for a few days before I moved into accommodation that the British Council had reserved for us. For the first week or so that I lived with my parents I enjoyed my mother's home cooking. A week later I attended a two-week course that the British Council had organised for us. The course was designed to introduce students to life in the United Kingdom and I found it useful and informative.

I had a friend, Dr Mary Egerton, who was like a mother to me. I first met her when she was the Obstetrician at the Princess Christian Mission (Maternity) Hospital in Freetown Sierra Leone. She taught me about many of the things to do and not to do in Britain. I spent many weekends with her. During the first weekend I spent with her we went to Church early on the Sunday morning. On our way back we stopped at the newsagents to get Sunday newspapers. She asked me to take the one I would like to read. At that time I had no knowledge of British newspapers, so when I saw the paper *News of the World* I took it, believing that it would give me news about the whole world. Dr Egerton paid for it without saying a word. It was later after lunch as we sat to read the papers that she said "Belmont, that is the lowest Sunday newspaper you can buy". I felt very embarrassed and I never touched that paper again until I was in my final year at Medical School when we were having the lectures in forensic medicine. To my greatest surprise I heard the Professor say, "Your best textbook in forensic medicine is the *News of the World*!"

NEWS OF THE WORLD

During my first spring in England, Dr Egerton used to take me out for walks in the woods and we would spend a couple of hours picking primroses, pretty small yellow flowers that grow wild. I always found these walks inspiring and refreshing.

During my first two years in England I was a student at the Technical College in Brighton where I studied for the General Certificate of Education at Advanced Level. During the time that I was in Brighton, an English woman called Rose, aged 83 years, extended to me an open invitation to tea on Sunday afternoons with her family. On the second Sunday I visited she said to me, "You will be a good doctor because you are a good listener". I have always been thankful to Rose, of blessed memory, for making me become aware of the importance of being a good listener. During that time, I lived in lodgings with an English family on part-board, that is, room with breakfast and evening meal Monday to Friday, and lunch as well at weekends.

I did experience a few unpleasant incidents during my first years in England. They were related mainly to landladies who would say they had a room when I spoke to them on the telephone, but when I arrived on their doorsteps, only a few minutes later, and they saw I was black, they would immediately say, "Sorry, the room has been taken."

I subsequently studied Medicine at the University of Bristol Medical School. I was the only black female and there were just three male students from Nigeria in my year at Medical School. I was very lucky in that several female English students invited me to spend holidays or weekends with their families. I got to know other parts of England and Wales, as most of them came from outside Bristol. Consequently I thoroughly enjoyed my student days at the University. I went to the cinema when there were good films and I saw many good shows and plays at the theatre.

After graduation I specialised in obstetrics and gynaecology, working in hospitals here in England. I am extremely grateful to my mother for teaching me to sew and to do embroidery. These were great assets when I was doing surgical operations. All the Consultants I worked

Belmont's needlework skills came in handy

with commented on the straightness of my incisions and the fact that I was able to do the various stitches we use in surgery with relative ease. I remember the first time a Consultant Surgeon asked me if I would like to put in a stitch during an operation I was assisting in as a student. Trembling, I said yes. As soon as I put in one stitch he asked me to put in another. He then said, "Do you do needlework, Belmont?" I said, "Yes". Then he said, "I knew that as soon as I saw you put in the first stitch". The Surgeon then went on to say that he used to sit on his grandma's footstool as she taught him to do the various stitches he would need to do in operations. On passing the exams, I became a Member of the Royal College of Obstetricians and Gynaecologists, by which time I was married and had a five-month-old daughter. I then returned home to Sierra Leone with my daughter.

I worked as an obstetrician and gynaecologist outside Freetown, the capital. My work brought me into contact with seriously ill newborns, infants and young children, as there wasn't a specialist paediatrician in that part of the country at that time. I soon discovered that the maternal mortality, that is death of women during pregnancy and childbirth, was very high, as were the death rates of newborns, infants and young children, and I could see that these deaths were largely preventable through good community nursing and education. This inspired me to go back to medical school and obtain a Postgraduate Degree in Public Health. As a result, when the Maternal and Child Health Division was established in the Ministry of Health in Sierra Leone, I was appointed its first Director. Working in that position, I initiated a programme to identify and train 'Traditional Birth Attendants.' These were village women who looked after mothers during pregnancy. So I spent most of my working life back in Africa, but still wanted to return to my family, now settled in England when I retired.

Mrs Josephine Macpeppele Ja Ja

I moved around a lot when I first came over to England. First I lived in Kilburn, and then my mother and I rented a room in West Hampstead. Then we moved into a house which my husband had taken in Camden Town. He rented out rooms there to help pay for it. My husband was very possessive and got jealous if I spoke to anyone, especially men. He thought I had done bad things with them. He used to worry every time I went out and tried to stop me. I was taking tablets to help me cope with his rages and my mother thought it was because of worry over the children. But then she found out it wasn't because of them at all; it was because of the way my husband was treating me, so we got divorced. The council found me a house in Kennington and I moved in there with my mother and the children.

I got a job at Euston train station cleaning the carriages. I also went to evening classes at the Polytechnic in the Edgware Road and learned how to sew. Then I got work repairing theatrical costumes. I really enjoyed working there; the people were really friendly. The staff were mixed, white and black working together, and I had no problems there.

Then my mother became sick and she wanted to go back to Nigeria, so I went with her. I left the children here with my husband. Their schooling was here, so

I couldn't just take them away. He was a good father too, but a bit dominating. My own father had passed away when we returned. We lived in a place called Port Harcourt. They had opened a hairdressers in the Presidential Hotel, so I got a job there doing the European hair styles. Then I decided to set up a small beauty parlour of my own nearer my home, because of the long distance to go to the hotel.

I returned to England because I wanted to see my daughter. She was getting married, and then she had a baby so I stayed with her. I had to return to Nigeria after a while because our house had been burnt down during the civil war there. The Nigerian government gave us another house, but they didn't complete it, so we had to finish it off with our own hands. I lived there for some time and just came on holiday to England when I could. I was travelling back and forth, but this was difficult, because each time it involved travelling all the way from the East of Nigeria, where we lived, to Lagos in the west and that was a very long distance. The authorities were beginning to be suspicious of me because I was travelling back and forth so much, but I wasn't a troublemaker. I was really stressed by the situation and I ended up having a stroke. My sons came over, one after another, to help me in Nigeria, but it was all too strenuous for them, because by then they had their own families in England. So eventually I returned to England to stay.

Mr Ade Aderogba

It was cloudy when I reached Liverpool. I think it was either raining or about to rain. The immigration people who met us just counter-stamped my student visa and gave me two years as a student. They warned me not to exceed this time. I should renew my visa if I had any reason to stay for longer and I could apply to do this at the Home Office.

There was nobody to meet me in Liverpool. I was travelling straight to London by train and I had the address of a relative in Camberwell. I found my way to his house, where he was waiting for me. He and his wife had a spare room where I could stay. He was working for Haywards pickle factory in Rotherhithe, south-east London, so he was able to get me a job there too. My job was to turn the small Italian onions and pickled gherkins over in the barrels. If the barrels were left for a long time, the onions started rotting, so you had to keep turning these heavy big barrels over, and that was my job. I was in the shed, not the main factory. I did that for a few weeks because I wanted to earn a bit of money to send to my family and I wasn't going to start my studying until September.

They were men who had left school as fifteen-year-olds and some of them were ex-dockworkers in London and so on, cockneys mostly. I was the only black man. Every Friday they got their pay. I remem-

Ade's mother "bonded beautifully" with his wife

ber the second Friday I was there, one of them said I should go with them to the pub. Well, back home we didn't take our pay on a Friday and walk straight into a bar and start drinking. No, we went home and changed and played tennis, then maybe had a beer later. My friends in the factory wanted to take me to what I thought they were calling 'tough accountants' (meaning 'turf accountants') and I said, "who are they?" And they said, "they are betting shops," and I said "What? I have never been to a betting shop in my life." So they found me to be an oddity, and they questioned me on how I didn't know any swear words but knew so much about English history. If I started to talk about the Battle of Hastings and the Norman Conquest, they said, "What is all this that is coming out of your head? Who put all that into your head? " And I said, "My English teachers back home in the Colonies."

I had seen an advert in *The Guardian* for an Assistant Accountant with Camden Council and I went for the job and got it. I went back and told my friends in the factory and they said, "We're not surprised. You know you don't really belong here."

I stayed with my friend in Camberwell for about three to four months, and then I rented my own room nearby. It belonged to an Ananuga Nigerian man, and I said that is my tribe, Ananuga, Yoruba. He asked me for a deposit and he gave me the key and showed me the gas meter. He said, "If you don't want to be cold you have to put some coins in the meter."

I met my future wife while I was working at Camden. We got married in 1967 in Hampstead Town hall. Then I took a one-year postgraduate course at Exeter University and my darling wife gave up her post in Camden Council and came with me to Devon, taking a fairly junior job in Devon County Council Planning Department.

There was civil war in Nigeria, and I knew that as soon as I finished my course at Exeter, I would go back to Africa. I sailed back to Nigeria on a cargo boat in July

1968, and my wife came with me. We stayed for a while with my brother who was a hospital administrator. Then he said, "I can't continue to feed you two forever – you must get a job! You've got good qualifications". So he spoke to his friend, who was head of one of the Ministries, and I was given a job as personnel manager of the first paper industry in Nigeria. Until then, Nigeria, a country of 100 million people, had imported every scrap of paper. The Germans had built this factory, but it had been abandoned during the civil war because the Germans were thought to be implicated on the Ibo side and they had been forced to leave. My job was to recruit over 1,000 staff, put in the management, design the system and get it going. And within six months we were in production, producing paper. And from there, I got head-hunted and given employment with the World Bank. So I worked for the World Bank Group for sixteen years, in Africa.

My wife adapted remarkably well to life in Africa, apart from a bout of malaria. She bonded beautifully with my mum and my relatives. My children were born in Nigeria. My mum, my brothers and my sister were all very fond of my children and they accepted my wife absolutely. That's why she was there for nearly 20 years.

But when the children reached the age of eleven, we came over to look at boarding schools in England. I didn't want anything in the south of England, you know, because there were all kinds of problems. So I went for Yorkshire, and I saw this beautiful boarding school. It was a Quaker school called Ackworth in Pontefract. It was 200 years old, for boys and girls and it had excellent facilities. And in 1981, when my eldest was 11, I put him on the plane, "I don't want to go!" "You gotta go, boy!". He came for seven years, O-levels, A-levels. And his brother joined him, and then Lola, my daughter joined. So all three of them went to the same co-ed boarding school, and then they all went on to medical school – Liverpool Medical School, Bristol Medical School and Leicester Medical School. All three are doctors.

I don't think my children have suffered racism through being of mixed race. None of them has ever come to me to say this. My eldest son was the first black boy to be school captain in hockey, and that says a lot. You know, when they went to boarding school there were not too many blacks, but they were very active in all aspects of the school, and they came to Nigeria when they weren't in boarding school, three times a year, for the holidays of course. Colour-wise it's never really been much of a problem. And it has helped them in their careers because intellectually they operate at a different level, having both cultures.

My wife was there in Nigeria for nineteen years, almost twenty years. She came back in 1987 because one of us had to be there for the kids, especially in the school holidays, and I followed in 1989.

We bought a house in Nottingham, and she got a job straight away at the University of Derby. She was never jobless for one day, you know. So we settled in Nottingham. But Nottingham is a very English town – no blacks. The few Asians are cab drivers, and I couldn't talk to them. I was lonely. I was sitting in front of the telly watching *Home & Away*. And one day my wife saw me looking at my photographs of my relatives back home, and she said, "You're a bit lonely and homesick, aren't you? We met in London. We have many friends in London. If you want to go back and do something in London, you are free." So I was allowed to come back to London and I worked here until my retirement.

Mr James Adebayo Adesina
I had arranged to live with a friend in Tufnell Park, so I had somewhere to go when I arrived. It was a damp basement, not a healthy environment, but I survived. There were three of us living there and we were all students. After I had settled in, I went to sort out my course. I went to Brixton School of Building to do a full time course. I liked the course and I got settled fairly quickly. It was good living in London too, because I could be together with people of my own kith and kin. Some Nigerians tried living outside London, but eventually they returned because people seemed unfriendly outside London.

In London too there was prejudice, especially when you were looking for a room; you came up against a blank wall. "Sorry, no coloureds", "No niggers" and we had never been confronted with that type of discrimination. We didn't have much interaction with English people in my area.

My experience here was very different to what I had been taught during our etiquette lessons. I think the more you tried that, the more you lost your identity completely. Because no matter what you do, those that will not be satisfied will never be satisfied. A nasty experience I had was that in the house I was in, there was no bathroom. I liked to take a bath everyday, even sometimes two times. And when I told my host I wanted a bath, he said, "Bath? You are joking? We take a bath once a week, and we go to a place where we buy a ticket like this in the public baths and we stay there until we are called out." And you wouldn't believe what sort of dirt you will have after not taking a bath for a week – it's unbelievable!

There were are few of us living in one room in a shared house. That room was your bedroom, sitting room and kitchen, everything. To heat the room we used a paraffin heater and it was very dangerous. Everyone did different shifts, so the lodgers who came home in the morning would put the heater on to warm up or use it too cook rice. Sometimes my flatmates who worked the nightshift dozed off whilst cooking the rice and it would spill over. This was very dangerous as the rice would burn or the gas would ooze out while people are sleeping.

There was not much spare time because you had to study for the course. I think that most of us from Nigeria found it difficult to do technical drawing because we were not actually brought up with engineering drawing skills, so on Saturday, we spent time practicing these things with a drawing board. Physics, chemistry, mechanics, mathematics were subjects we learned thoroughly, so there wasn't much time to socialise; only during the holidays, when we went to parties and saw friends that were getting married. We had had the opportunity of meeting people from Kenya, Uganda, Somalia, Sudan, Tanzania especially at college, but most important, people from your own background.

Then my wife came in 1962. I was delighted when I knew she was coming. I got a job. My first job was with the contractors, Waites Builders in Norbury. They posted me to Richmond in Surrey, to one of their giant estate developments. And I worked there for about six months. I then decided to resign and went to do a course at Bournemouth College of Technology for three years. After my course had finished, I decided to move back to London, and I worked for Lambeth Council.

I decided to go back to Nigeria in July 1971. I didn't want to stay in this country. I had done the training and I thought I would be much more useful to my own native country, and there was an opportunity because we had gained our independence. So I decided to go back to Nigeria. Many of my friends and relatives had already gone back home ahead of me from 1969 onwards. All my family over there were looking forward to seeing me, and they were so delighted when I returned after eleven years of staying in foreign lands. I was welcomed. And then I looked for a job and I started working. And I trained my children there. And then I had another three children in Nigeria. I had six children, one of the set of my children are twins – a boy and a girl. Three were born here three were born in Nigeria. I started my own business, but unfortunately, due to the unstable military government, my business in engineering work was affected. So I decided to return to Britain.

Mrs Mako Herabe

I came to Britain in 2001. My daughter Faduma met me at Heathrow airport. It was such a relief to see her because we had been separated for five years. I couldn't believe she was standing in front of me. I was just crying. Before I arrived I had to organise so much paperwork. You have to send all your papers to the Ethiopian embassy and they will send papers back to Home Office. They say, "Yes we confirm that this person has this status," and then the family reunion can go ahead. They take pictures and do visas, papers, passports so no one will question where you are going and who will support you when you get there. I had the papers ready, but when I reached 'arrivals' I couldn't write or read. Anyway, no-one stopped me, so I just followed the other people. I was expecting a long delay before I saw my daughter, but she was there waiting for me.

Mrs Hawa Ismail Mumin

I came in 1996, I have been here eight years. I had fled to Nairobi because life in Somalia was so unstable, all my children had fled to different places but my daughter had come to Britain. I wanted to join her so I was helped by the Red Cross. I was very lucky because many people were using different routes to flee Somalia, crossing borders and waiting to hear from family. I eventually heard news from my daughter and arrangements were made for me to come and settle in London.

I didn't have any idea of how different from home London would be. It was winter time when I arrived I saw that all the trees had no leaves. The first thing I asked my daughter was where are the leaves. Back home you relied on green leaves, so I thought if the trees are like this how do these people live? What do they eat? Back in Somalia, green leaves represent wealth because the livestock are fed and milk is produced. I found it very strange that food was frozen but my daughter explained the seasons and how food was cultivated and preserved in Britain.

CARIBBEAN ELDERS

Mrs Hyacinth Thomas

My first job when I came to London was doing the bag wash in an old-fashioned launderette. People brought all their clothes in one big bag and they were sorted – whites from coloureds – and they were washed. It was a nasty job because I don't think people cared what they put into the bag. It was the first time I knew that bugs were in England as well!

My second job was at Peak Freans biscuit factory. It was a full time job. I think I was on washing and stacking the tins. I think they paid you a standard wage but you could earn more according to how quick you were – like piecework. I earned more than my boyfriend used to earn. I can remember the first time I worked there in the evening – part time, 5.00 – 10.00 at night. I used to stuff myself with biscuits. During the day they were black and white working together, but in the evenings just whites, until that changed in about 1968. I was a hard worker. I got the job as an evening person. And I met one other black woman there. More and more came afterwards to do the evening shift. In the late sixties we used to meet at weekends, go to one another's house and have a party. That's how we used to enjoy ourselves. I think I went to the cinema once when the cinema was over the road.

I said I would only be here for five years and now I am here for forty. Although we had always been taught that England was our mother country, I personally felt, "This is not my country – I'm not here to stay." We would ignore things – racist things, which nowadays the youngsters aren't going to ignore because they see themselves as British through and through.

We introduced people here to green banana and yam and pumpkin and all the exotic fruits. In the sixties you'd never see anything like that so you used to hanker for getting back home to go wild on some of those things. But now you get more here than you can get in the West Indies. They earn more by exporting than they actually earn by selling to the natives.

I went back to the West Indies for the first time in 1971. It was exciting. At that time I had my third child; she was seven years old when I took her back. It was nice her meeting her grandmother for the first time and all her aunties, going to the beach, and having a picnic on the beach. All of us used to like going in the forest – the bush. And you'd sleep out in tents or in caves. You'd cook and eat in the open air. Then there were the wonderful carnivals where you would dress in beautiful coloured costumes and dance in the streets.

Mrs Irma Reid

My sister Christiana and I arrived at Southampton in March. We got the train to London and the sun was really bright and it was hot through the train windows. We thought this is like Trinidad, it is really nice and warm, and we couldn't understand why it was so cold when we got outside, even though the sun was still shining. Luckily we had these coats that I had made so we wore them all the time.

I could not believe it when I saw all the houses were joined up together and all with chimneys and smoke coming out of them. It looked picturesque, like little dolls' houses, you know, like what you see in the postcards. And the people were strange as well. They were nothing like we

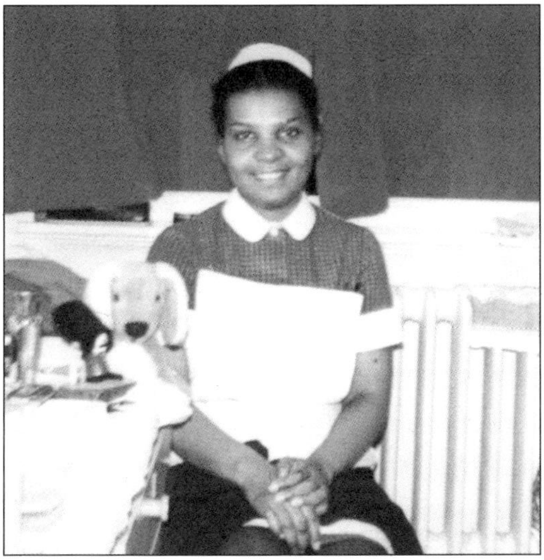

expected. Sometimes you'd speak to people and they wouldn't answer you. It was as if you were speaking a different language or they just didn't want to talk to you. But as for actual prejudice, well we never experienced racial prejudice when we were here.

We had to find our way to the hospital where we would be working in Grove Park, South London. Christiana and I had heavy suitcases and we had bought extra things and souvenirs on the way, when the boat stopped in Lisbon. When we reached Grove Park station, we came out with our heavy suitcases and the bags and said to the chap who was collecting the tickets, "Can you tell us where Grove Park Hospital is, so we can take a bus or a taxi?" He said, "No you don't need either. It's just round the corner." So we set off, not realising what a long way it was going to be, lugging our heavy cases. We walked and we walked, and when we finally reached the hospital and we looked up at it, Christiana and I we were scared; we felt as if we were going to prison. The hospital wall was about ten feet high, a red brick wall and, on top of the wall, they had barbed wire and a big heavy iron gate. It reminded me of the prisons back in Trinidad.

We went through and there was a little porter's cabin and the chap went and got the home warden. She took us to our rooms. I had thought that Christiana and I would be sharing, but they put us in two rooms next to each other. That was frightening because back home we always shared a room. We went up the lift to these rooms which were like little box rooms. We had a cupboard to put our things in. And then she showed us the bathroom. We were used to showers and we didn't like the idea of having the same dirty water on your skin when you have soaped and washed yourself. We thought it was horrible. She showed us where the kitchen was, downstairs, but we were not allowed to cook, only to make tea. She showed us where the canteen was, where we had to go and eat there.

I remember the first meal was roast beef and potato and peas. I took a salad as well and the woman behind the counter says, "Oh you can't have two meals, you either have the salad or you have the beef." And I am saying, "But this is not a meal; this is just salad." She said "Oh well, you have one or the other, you can't have both." So I had to leave the salad. There was salt on the table and pepper, but there was no pepper sauce or anything like that to put on it, so to us the food was absolutely tasteless. We began to miss home, especially when we had to go to bed in our own separate rooms. We felt like we were locked in prison.

We first went to Preliminary Training School. We were there Monday to Friday and we had Saturday and Sundays off. When we actually started work on the wards, we worked 42 hours a week. Then there was what they used to call the 'awful shift', which involved working from seven o' clock in the morning till one, then again from five until eight at night. That was called awful because, when you finished work at one o' clock, you couldn't do anything or go anywhere because you had to be back in time.

After two years I qualified as nurse. I also did a cardio-thoracic course which I combined with my State-Enrolled Nurse (SEN) training. In those days, tuberculosis was still prevalent, so I trained to nurse patients with tuberculosis, or chronic heart disease and chest problems. At the end of my training, I didn't want to stay on at that hospital, although I had enjoyed myself there once I settled in. Somebody told me I could do agency nursing, but what I didn't realise was that our visas only allowed us to work as hospital employees, so

by doing agency nursing I was breaking the rule. When I joined the Nursing Agency, they placed me in Tadworth Hospital, in Surrey near Epsom. I was working there early one morning when the Matron called me and Christiana up to the office and told us that they heard from the Home Office that we were not supposed to be working there through an agency and we would have to leave.

We decided that we would go home in December, because we had been here for two years already. We wanted to go and see our parents over Christmas and then come back after a few weeks to start work in January. Before we left, Christiana and I applied for work inside the hospital system so we would have jobs to come back to and we got our acceptance letters (which we would be able to take to the Home Office) the day before we were due to leave.

Mr Michael Roper

I came over by ship in 1951 when I was twenty years old. For me it was an adventure. I was very sea sick until I arrived in Dover. I got on the train to London, Charing Cross. Then my aunt came down to meet me to take me to her house in Kentish Town. I asked her, "Where is the ocean?" She replied, "What do you mean? There is no ocean in London." Back home, there was a big yard round every house and beyond that, the bluest of oceans. My aunt told me I would get used to it. She took me to the shops. They were so little, I went in and asked for something and the shop-keeper said "What?" I said "You heard what I said. I don't like repeating myself." I had to get used to so many things.

I lived in my aunt's house. She had an illness and had to go into hospital. She wanted me to take care of the house and collect the rent from her African tenants while she was in hospital. I worked from the day my aunt went into hospital until I retired. I never stopped working. I was making hearing aids. We made every type of hearing aid and fixed them as well. I managed to make £6 a week, which I thought was not bad money. There were two of us doing this job. Then one day, there was a new manager put in and he gave me the sack. He was unpopular and almost everybody walked out. I started to look for other jobs I ended up making electronic devices and time switches. My company had a contract with the government, and the BBC used them. You set them up to switch on automatically in the morning. Then I did television repairs.

I never had any trouble through being black. Everyone was really friendly to me. There was one bloke who said to me, "Why do they keep troubling me?" I said, "Who is troubling you?" He told me that when he walked down the street, and he saw a white person he felt like there was going to be trouble. I replied "What are you saying? No white man ever do me any thing in England. As long as you don't trouble them, they don't trouble you. I go any place I want, and I talk to them, just the same as anyone else." I've never been back to the Caribbean in all the years I've been here, though I did always write to my mother while she was alive.

Mrs Gladys Smith

I came into Folkestone by ship in 1960. I was never a person to get into the thick of things, you know, I like to stand back and see things go smoothly, I can't rush or fight my way, I never did. So with this crowd on the boat, you have no idea what it was like, with about six or seven hundred people, all rushing to make their way through. At one time, coming off the ship, I am sure I wasn't standing on the ground, the way they were pushing, you know? They almost lifted me off the ground!

I was the last person to come off that ship and get through customs. I just stood back and waited and said, "Well, we'll all be seen to." And when I got through, almost everybody had gone and there was nobody to meet me. Oh it was grim! It was August and it was a damp evening and I was all alone. I got to London by train and a friendly person organised a taxi to take me to where my cousin lived. I'd never seen houses built like this, these attached houses, and I didn't know which was my cousin's flat. I didn't dare to ring the bell or call out, because I didn't know how many people I would have been disturbing. I just sat in that little porch for three hours, from three o'clock in the morning until six o'clock. I knew that he would be moving about then, because he was working on London Transport, on the trains, so at six o'clock he would be getting ready to leave. So at six o'clock I rang the bell. My cousin was so surprised that I was there. He had called the day before to find out the movements of the ship I was on and was told that they had no word when it would be in and he should call again the next day. At the time he called, I was actually already in Folkestone! Now he was checking to see how soon he could call for news of the ship, and all that time I was on his doorstep.

My first memory of snow was that heavy snow in 1962. I went to bed one evening and the following morning, when I opened the curtain, I saw the whole place covered white and the snow was still falling. I was so elated, oh my! I was running from one end of the house to the next, just to see the snow falling! I was so glad to see it, and even now I love to see that snow falling.

ASIAN ELDERS

Mr Santi Rakhit

It was very grey and foggy when I first came over. I thought, why am I staying here in this cold place? My brother was living here. He and another friend came to receive me. And they took me to a café in Marble Arch for sausages and chips! So I said, "What is this?", they replied "It's a hot dog," and I said, "I can't eat dog!"

My brother's friend took me to his house and he searched for some rice and lentils which he'd kept in an old suitcase for two or three years. He cooked the rice and lentils very well and the three of us ate. My brother knew what I needed and equipped me with the right clothes, but I was really freezing all the time. I stayed in my brother's flat at first.

I was amazed that people don't talk to

each other in this country! They didn't even say hello. They were all just sitting reading the paper! I thought, what's this? On the second day, I went to Trafalgar Square to see all the pigeons. And lots of lovely pictures in the National Gallery. Someone came up to me in Trafalgar Square and said, "Can I take your picture?" I said, "Yes, you can take a picture of me." I didn't know that I would have to pay money afterwards. So they took the pict- ure. I don't know how much he asked for. But I said, "Well, there's all the money I have!" I wondered if this was something dodgy. I went to my brother's friend and told him this had happened, and he said to call the police. So this policeman came up and heard my side of the story. He agreed that it shouldn't happen like that. In those days, anyone could take any photo- graph. I suspect it was my protest which initiated the license to take photographs in Trafalgar Square!

There were two more months to go before I was to start my studies. I visited all these poets' houses, and I went to see Wordsworth's house in the Lake District, which my teacher in India told me about.

When I came back to London, I visited the Indian Embassy, because some money was to be sent for me from India – I had some sort of scholarship, you see. And there was a job available there, working in the Embassy. I said, "Well, that's a thought. If I could work and study, it would be a good thing. I wouldn't have to depend on my parents, or anybody else. And straight away I filled the form in and was interview- ed by a Miss Moss. I got in at the Embassy. And when the time came to study, I stayed on, combining the job and studying.

My brother's flat was a long way from Central London. It was very difficult for me to commute to the Indian Embassy. Luckily, I got to know a chap who was also at the Indian Embassy and he said, "I know somebody I can introduce you to." He spoke to this friend, who was a land- lady, and he invited her over with her husband and he cooked her a meal. Then

I went to their house. I think they were quite nervous about taking me in at first, but at that time I was quite handsome, with a nice little face! In those days, for a family like them to take an Indian boy into their house was quite a big thing.

They were so nice, and in the family there were two doctors (the brother-in-law and the sister) and my landlord was an engineer at Plessy International company. One of the brothers was a colonel in the army in India, so they had an interest in all things Indian. I was looked after like their own son. It was the best time of my life. I had never lived so comfortably, even in my own home. And they didn't have any children, so I really became their child. Some Sundays, when I used to go to see my brother – they used to have a Sunday roast you see – and they used to save some for me until I came back later!

Time went on, and then perhaps around this time I went back to India. I still had my job at the Embassy, you see, I had a good job and it was difficult to give the job up. So my older brother said, "Yes, it's okay with us that you go back to England, but are you willing to get married first? If you get married, it's okay. Get married, go, and we won't worry about you anymore!" My parents would not let me come back to England without getting married! No, you see, in India it happens like that. An arranged marriage is something you need. Family ties, connections, status of the family, which family you come from. You get matched together. Then they decide whether you would be a good match or not. Happy ever after – it was a good match for me! I brought my wife back with me to England. I came back and joined the embassy again and resumed my studies.

When I finished my accountancy training I wanted to gain some experience in industry in England with the thought of moving back to India eventually. So I joined GEC. I was in operational cost control there. Later, when the work prospects became very limited, I took the open competition to join the Home Civil Service. I worked in Whitehall in the Department of Health. It was such a lovely location to work in – fantastic surroundings! Every lunchtime I would walk all around the locality as far as possible, getting to know it.

I had my own office in Whitehall, working for the Ministry – Virginia Bottomley was then the Health Secretary. I was in the finance branch of the Department of Health in Whitehall, and I used to control the various financial activities of the Department of Health. Some people say there is a 'glass ceiling' and that people not born in Britain can't rise above a certain level in the Civil Service. I don't know how it happened for me, but maybe my teacher, my culture, my heritage all helped. Towards the end of my life's journey, I can say that I've settled happily in England with my family and we have many friends around us.

Mrs Avtar Bilkhu

When I arrived at Heathrow, I had to be interviewed. That was the only way I could be let in. There was an interpreter who spoke in Punjabi. They asked me about chest x-rays. I was very scared at that time, thinking they might not let me in. They gave me an injection because they thought I might be carrying cholera and small pox. They gave it to all the people from the villages. Once my examination was over, I reached arrivals. I didn't recognise my husband. He was clean shaven and no turban. He was working in a bakery and they did not accept turbans in those days. It is better now.

We took a taxi to my new home, a rented property in Plumstead. We were sharing the house with five other people. Then there was my father-in-law, two of my children and my husband and me, so altogether there were ten people living in this small house! My husband said to me, "Are you all right? Will you have cup of tea?" I said, "No, I'm tired and I don't feel like eating or drinking." I just slept. I will never forget that first day in England: my husband just went off to work. I hardly saw him as he was working day and night. When he was at home, he never talked to me in front of his father and he really didn't support me much when I first came over.

My children didn't even recognise their father, it had been so long since they had seen him. They kept saying, "Who is that man? Who is that man?" They didn't know him, and when he tried to touch the kids, they shouted, "Don't touch my arm".

Many Sikh men were forced to remove their turbans and shave their beards

Life here was worse than in India for me. At that time we had very little money. My husband was only earning £11 to £12 pounds a week. At that time I wasn't doing anything except taking care of the kids. I fell pregnant again and had two more children. When you have to think about the children, the food and buying clothes, it was very hard to make ends meet. So I started working from home sewing and making clothes. I slowly took up more work and made money. I had no social life, nothing. I would just take the children to school and come back to the same position at the sewing machine until 10 o'clock at night, still stitching, because it had to be finished by the morning. I decided to find another job. I worked in a butter factory for about four years. I even took up English classes at a local Convent school. The nuns were my teachers. I was very shy. I never even said hello to anyone. I wanted to learn because it was really difficult talking to my children who were born here.

Then I had an interview at the Asian Resource Centre and after that, I worked at lots of different places, such as the family planning clinic advising Asian women, and then I worked for Social Services. After working really hard for many years, my husband and I bought our first house.

I visited home every year, I really missed my family especially my uncle. He sadly passed away in Britain when he came over to visit. He wasn't keen to come because he was such a busy man working with the community in the village. He was involved in an accident at Shooters Hill. He had internal bleeding in the chest, and after ten days he died. He insisted I be there before he died. I put my hands over his eyes and he asked me to pray. He liked that. I was very sick for about three months after he died. I couldn't eat properly I was crying so much.

Mr Fazal Rahim Shah

I arrived at Heathrow and I had nowhere to go. When I came out, I asked the taxi driver to take me to a lodging house. The taxi driver took me from Heathrow to east London, to a family, and he said, "That house. Knock at the door." I knocked and said, "Have you got a room for me?", and the man said, "Yes". It was fifty pence, or in those days, ten shillings.

I didn't know the currency. So I gave him my £5 and he took the money, and he gave me some money back. I didn't know what the currency was – pounds, shillings and pence. I had one note of £5. I think he took £2 out of it, and gave me £2.50 or something back. He went up and showed me a room – just a basic room with no carpet. But fortunately for me, there were three rooms off that landing. The other two rooms were occupied by Pakistani boys, and they greeted me. And they said, "Don't worry. Until you are settled, you can eat with us". The house was occupied by single men, no families. They were young men, people like me who had come over a couple of years before.

And in those days, there never used to be a bathroom in the house. The first thing I asked was where I could go for a bath. And the boys told me, "Don't worry, we'll take you and show you where the baths are." There used to be big places for bathing provided by the council, at the end of the street, or at the end of the

block. This bath house was shared by everyone. I found this very strange because in Pakistan every household had their own bathroom and toilet. There was no concept of going out to take a bath. You had to take three pence and they would open up a cubicle and you could have a shower. They used to provide you with two towels, soap, everything!

The boys cooked a Pakistani meal. At that time I couldn't cook, but they were good cooks. They had been here a while, so they were all settled and they taught me how to cook and how to prepare a meal. In those days, it was not easy to cook an Asian meal. We could only afford meat once a week, and we didn't have a rolling pin or anything to make chapattis. We used the empty milk bottles to roll out the chapatti!

I was living in East End of London it was the hub of the Asian community – especially Bengalis. Not Pakistanis like me, but the Bengalis were there. They were the first arrivals, and we were the second batch. And they gave me a hand.

One day, I was going to the bath house, and there was a sign outside this handbag factory saying, "Dispatch clerk wanted." And I just went in, and said, "I want a job!" I had an interview but the interview was not like today, with a CV. That was unheard of. You would just go in, and they would ask you what you can do. "Okay, start tomorrow!" That's how job interviews worked. I was very excited. I thought I was lucky because I found this job the third day after arriving in London. I didn't even ask, "How much are you going to pay me?" He didn't ask me any questions, he just said I should start on Monday. At the end of the week, he paid me, I think, £6. And after he'd taken the tax and everything, he gave me £5 I was very happy. £5 was a lot of money. I paid ten shillings for the room, and the rest of the money was left for me to spend.

My job was to see to the orders. I checked through the book, made the invoice and delivery note. I labelled them, and then the truck used to come and collect the orders and take then to the different shops. But I didn't want to do that indefinitely. I wanted to go into the factory, and learn how to make bags. I had wanted to study when I first came over, but I knew I would have to earn some money first. I thought I'd find a job and then enroll at the local college, but I soon realised that I couldn't mix work and study together. So I stuck with the job, taking much more interest in it. I started doing different things in the factory, besides my own work. I said to myself, "Let's go through this channel and see what happens". I wanted to learn a skill.

The creation of a handbag was fascinating and challenging for me. In those days you had to learn all the skills – everything that goes into making a bag. You become a master craftsman, and then you design. I asked my boss, "I want to go into the factory and learn the skill." He said, "Yes, you can go into the other departments when you have finished your daily work". And he used to give me a day's work, and I used to save an hour or two hours at the end of it to go to the factory and learn machining, cutting, framing... everything! But then, the next day he would give me two hours work extra to make up for it, so I had to work very hard. Over two or three years that I worked there, I became very expert. I used to start at eight o'clock, and finish at half-past five. And I used to finish my own job at about three, half-past three, and the rest of the time I used to go into the factory and learn how to do things. Machining was one thing, cutting was the most important thing – hand cutting it used to be – to know what the bag is like.

There was no such thing as telephoning home. Well there was a telephone, but it was expensive, so I would write. When I told my father what I was doing, he didn't mind that I was not studying. I used to save money and send it home, because my father had paid 1,792 rupees for my fare. I told my mother that I would pay them back, and so I kept on sending my mother and father extra money. Then I had four sisters and I used to send enough for them to get married.

After work I was so tired, because we had to come home, cook meals, eat, and by that time there isn't much time until the next morning when you had to get up early. Saturday and Sunday were the two days off. Saturday all the boys used to dress up and go to the movies – an Indian movie. This was our weekly routine. From there we would just come home and have a meal at somebody's house. There were no Indian restaurants in those days and we couldn't afford to eat out. Someone cooked a meal, and we would talk about the film and have a chat. The letters from home were not so frequent. The letters used to take fourteen days to arrive. So if a friend got a letter from home, that was a big occasion. We all wanted to know what was happening back home. On Sunday I was washing, cleaning the house, writing letters. I would read books and magazines, things like that. There was not much spare time. No time to have a girlfriend. We never even thought about having a female friend.

I worked in that factory for nine years in the same place. They made me a manager there and the boss became a very good friend of mine. And from there I opened up my own business while I was still working in the factory. At half-past five we all used to finish, but I had taken a room somewhere else, and I had started my own factory. But I was not sure whether I would be successful, because 99.9% of the trade was owned by Jews in those days, and there were no outsiders. And especially a coloured immigrant from Pakistan starting up in a line which was entirely run by Jews was unheard of. But within a year or two, I had one of the biggest manufacturing bases in the East End. My business was called Collis Handbags, and I had thirty-seven people working for me. And I was supplying for Manchester, Glasgow, everywhere! I was about 32 years old by then.

Mrs Pramila Desai

When I reached Heathrow, my husband and some other relatives were there to greet me. The plane was one hour late. Everyone was very worried and they were very relieved to see me. When I got off the plane it was very dark, it was miserable weather and very frosty. At that moment I thought, "Oh no, what a very bad country! India is so very bright and warm. I think this is a mistake."

We went first to my sister's house. She made some food and then we went to Blackheath Road in Greenwich where my husband owned a shop. He was studying, and working in the cinema, but his friend needed someone to help him run the shop so my husband agreed and became a partner. It was a grocery shop and we lived above the shop. It was just my husband and me. It was large shop and there were six rooms upstairs. I found it all a bit strange. There was a little room where my husband was cooking and you know men don't keep the room tidy, so it looked very depressing. For two or three days I cried every day. I was missing my family and friends. I felt strange and shy when I came out to serve the customers. I had very long hair and it was the custom to put flowers in the hair and wear new saris but it seemed out of place here. I remember one old lady said to me, "Why do you kill the flowers? You shouldn't kill the flowers. You should put them in a pot." My husband said "This is our custom", but I never wore flowers again.

People used to laugh at me because I couldn't pronounce the words. I only knew a little bit of English. Then, when I was pregnant with my first son, I had to go to the bank in Deptford one day. I was feeling very faint and collapsed because of my diabetes, but I couldn't communicate. All I could say was "my husband's shop." I fainted, and a man called the ambulance to take me to the hospital, but it just so happened that my husband was passing. Luckily he saw me and came over. I was taken to Greenwich Hospital and they kept me in for a while. I realised then that if I wanted to stay in this country, I needed to learn English. I started to learn through an old lady called Anne. She was a retired teacher who came into the shop and spoke English with me.

My husband sold mostly English and West Indian food like bananas and yams because there was a factory nearby which employed West Indians. The first time they came in the shop, I was frightened. I had never in my life seen big, tall, black people. Sometimes I dreamed at night-time that these people will come and kill me! I was afraid because I had never seen black people in India. I wasn't afraid of white people, but I was worried about how I could communicate with them. I was sad and very lonely.

It was very difficult raising children here. Whenever they were sick, I always missed my mum because there was no one to help me. At that time we had one old man living in the shop. He was a very nice man and he used to bring the medicine. Then a friend of my husband's came over from India with his wife and they invited me, so I made a new friend. Later, when these friends of my husband came for dinner, they saw we had space. The wife suggested that I put a cooker in one of the rooms and they could stay with us for a while. We agreed that they should

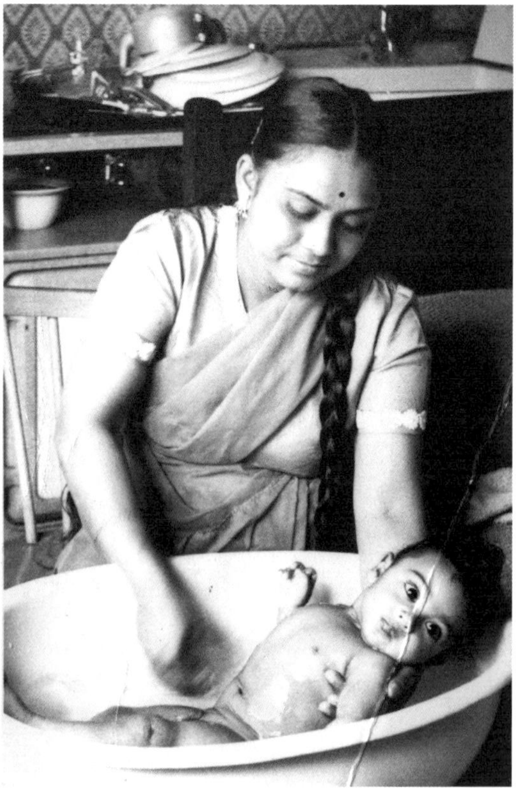

move in with us and she and her family lived with us for four years. We became good friends and then I stopped pining for India. She spoke very good English, we shared the care of our children and I began to move forwards.

I still wrote to my family often and I would wait for the post every day. I never visited India for about 32 years. In that time both my parents and my brother passed away. We went back to find a bride for my son because he was keen to get married in India.

I lived on Blackheath Road for 11 years

but then the trade went down because a huge Tesco's supermarket opened nearby so we had to bring the prices down. The old man who was living with us suggested that my husband find a job and that I run the shop by myself as I was a lot more confident now. So my husband went to work for the post office. The shop was still losing business and, as my husband was earning better money, we sold the shop and we were able to move to my present house in 1972.

Mrs Sheila Rakhit

I spoke English, but I was not very fluent. I'd learned at school and college. I had a Master's degree in Philosophy and Psychology from the University of Dakka in what is now Bangladesh.

I received a good reception from my in-laws, who were already living in this country. I first went to stay with my husband's brother who had married an Austrian girl. When I first arrived, I climbed in his car, and when I looked through the window, I found the houses looked so small! And joined together tightly. Back home, the part I come from, the houses are more like bungalows and very spread out. So it all looked strange to me.

I was disappointed. It's difficult to say what I had been expecting? But obviously from the books I'd read about England, I thought I'd see very big houses, flashy cars, and lights, and all that.

The traffic looked a continuous stream of cars, buses, lorries, and all going so fast. I thought, is this a race or a competition, you know, who is going to be the first one? I found it quite powerful. Anyway, I remember very well, on my first day in London, we stopped and bought fish and chips from a fish and chip shop. I had fish and chips wrapped in newspaper. That shocked me, but it tasted all right. But I would have preferred rice and curry instead.

When I came here, I needed to adjust to many things, many situations, many circumstances which I had never met before. It was hard, I tell you. Back home we use various gestures to express our desires and wishes and likes and dislikes, and that's enough. So those extra formalities of "no thank you", and "yes please", were very tiring for me. But anyway, it didn't take me very long to realise that there was no escape from talking. It was no use to protest. I tried hard to do the right thing.

And at that time, my husband and I faced some racial discrimination. It was very strong in the early 1960s. For example, people shut their front doors when we rang the front doorbell to enquire about their 'room to let' advert. We just had to accept it quietly, but we came away feeling sad. The English landlady who took us was known to my brother-in-law, and that's the only reason we did get a room. It was difficult in those days, really, unless you had a connection.

First we lived in North London, in Kilburn, in a 'bedsit', as it's called. We did everything in one room – sitting, cooking, eating, sleeping! Toilet and bathroom were shared with some other tenants in the house. I used to feel so strange when anybody came to visit us, you know, because we were doing everything in one room, and I wasn't used to living like that back home, so I found that to accept all this was quite hard for me.

I felt quite cold as winter was coming. And one heater was not sufficient – even though it was only one room. So we thought we must buy a hot water bottle to take to bed, and that was a new experience for me.

Seeing the snow for the first time was a new experience for me. And I just thought, ooh, it's not a picture in a book – I'm really seeing snow! I could hardly contain my excitement, and I screamed. And the landlady came out and she said, "It's all right! It's all right!" And I think I was thinking of going out. And she said, "You can go out, but take an umbrella with you". And I thought, "An umbrella? But there's no rain or anything!"

The first time I made an attempt to cook curry was a disaster, though my husband helped me. The cooking smell filled the whole room, and we had to open the window, because we were so scared that the landlady would come and tell us off. And the room got so cold!

I remember our landlady used to stare at me after I had a bath. She used to look at my dripping wet, long hair, and maybe she used to wonder why this Indian lady takes a bath every day, and wets her hair. I think I should have told her that to take a bath every day, including wetting hair, is nearly like a ritual in India. We had to share the bathroom and we had to put money in the gas meter.

I found it quite difficult to go to the shops. I could not explain to the shopkeeper properly and clearly because of lack of fluency in spoken English. I had to point to show what I wanted, and I ended up buying many things that I did not need because I didn't want to keep saying no, not that one.

My first day of going on the tube by myself, to go to attend a course called 'Intensive Spoken English for Overseas Graduates' at the City Literature Institute, was a nightmare! I lost my way round the underground. But I thanked my parents for sending me to college, because I could read the English map, with the names of the tube stations. And, in the end, I could sort out my travel route to get back to my destination. I think I couldn't ask anybody anything for two reasons: one, for my lack of fluency in spoken English; and two, because nobody had time to stop and answer, or listen to me, because everybody was following the stream of running crowds.

I was a rather shy and introverted person, which is considered to be a virtue

for an Indian girl. Another thing I found strange was getting used to calling people by their first name, when they are my father's or mother's age. Because this would be really objectionable according to Indian customs. When I came here, I found it quite difficult to meet new people, or to go to many parties. I used to pretend to be unwell, and avoided going to those parties. And one such occasion I remember, when I was asked to go to a Christmas dinner party, I was getting anxious how I was going to refuse when I would be offered an alcoholic drink, or eat using a knife and fork. So once there was an opportunity for me to go to the Queen's garden party with my husband – arranged through the High Commission of India. But I foolishly made excuses not to go. Now I would do anything, go to any lengths to get such an invitation!

For the next few years, my life was very busy, and hard. There was the pleasure of motherhood and the hectic life it brought, but there were very few Indian families living near us and we were very isolated. I realised then how important it is to have an extended family, which I would have had back home and which I missed. And how I wished to go back home to my mother and to other relatives to get all this help, you know, with the children. I was beginning to feel very tired and weary.

It was hard for my children too, to feel that they were the same as other children. I made myself go and talk to other parents at the school gate. But sometimes I didn't have enough confidence for this, I must admit. By then we had moved to South London. We lived in quite a mixed area, called Brockley, but there were not so many Indians. And I think also that among the white population, there was quite a lot of poverty in that area. So they were a bit resentful towards us, I felt.

I did take my children back home when they were little and I'm glad I did, even though it was very difficult to find the money in those days. That way, they came to meet my mother and their other grandparents. I did think of bringing my mother over here, but I did not have the money and the facilities to make her comfortable here. She died at 72, quite young, and I still find it hard to believe she's not there any more. I was not there when she died and that is a missing part of my life that I'll never get back.

Later on, as a mother, in order to fulfil my responsibilities as best I could, I had to sacrifice many comforts of my life. I think we didn't have a proper holiday for many years. But I don't regret it. The children are successful and have taken up worthwhile professions. They are both doctors now.

In between I joined a teacher's training college, to do a one-year course for graduates at Goldsmiths College. That was quite hard as well, you know. Most of them were young white girls, and I was an Indian mature woman. It was quite challenging, but I was successful. Following that, I taught for nearly twenty years, sometimes part-time, in primary schools, mainly in Southwark, Tower Hamlets and Lewisham. I had to overcome many hurdles during that period. I wore my saris to go to my school and maintained an image of myself as an Indian lady. I was not shy about wearing western clothes, but it was important for me in those days to keep our tradition. There were not many Indian teachers and not all of them wore Indian dress. The kids used to look and stare at me and that was a challenge, but I didn't get any abuse. I used to take time to explain to the children that this was my traditional dress. I was involved with multicultural education in schools and it was important for me to show them and explain things to them.

Settling Down Creative Activities

OLDER PEOPLE'S ACTIVITIES

Long-Distance Husbands & Fathers

Some couples had been apart for up to four years before being reunited in Britain. Do you remember your hopes and fears for the marriage when you arrived here in Britain? How did your children react to long-lost fathers? Can you write or say some of the things you felt at the time, and probably were not able to share with any one.

My First Room

Ask the older people where they lived when they first came to Britain. Ask them to draw a small floor plan to show you what they had in their first flat or room and how many people were sharing with them.

Longing for Home Cooking

When some of the story-tellers first came it was difficult to find familiar foods to cook. Cooking was often in a shared kitchen, so they had to wait for others to finish before they could begin. What foods and spices did the group members miss most when they came and how did they adapt to the difficult situation of cooking for themselves in an over-crowded space?

Any Work I Could Get

Many people had to take jobs well below their skill levels when they first arrived. Was this also true for members of the group? Ask people to share their memories of their early work experiences in this country.

Language Barriers

Many people had language problems and could only mix with people from their own country. How many members of the group tried to learn English when they came to Britain and how far did they progress? How much of a problem has this been in their daily lives here? See how many languages the group speak altogether and list them.

The Room Had Mysteriously Gone

Racism was sometimes not overt, but nevertheless people knew there was discrimination, especially over the matter of housing. Ask members of the group to share experiences of being accepted or refused as tenants and how they coped with this situation. Maybe ask two or three of the group to act out a memory.

YOUNG PEOPLE'S ACTIVITIES

This Is Your Father

Some of our story-tellers were bringing children who had not seen their fathers and would have to get to know them in this strange country. Can you speak out loud some of the thoughts of these children who were going to see their fathers for the first time? If each person says one line, the class can make a joint poem around these feelings.

A Changed Person?

Some husbands had had to adapt their clothes and hairstyles to meet British regulations so they looked quite different. From Mrs Avtar Bilkhu's story can you draw a picture of her husband before he left India and how he looked when she arrived in England some years later.

Paved with Gold?

One noticeable theme is people's surprise and often disappointment when they arrived in Britain. Brought up on English history, culture and literature, many immigrants were shocked to find dirt and poverty in Britain. Their expectations of streets paved with gold were far from fulfiled and they often had to settle for accommodation in the poorest parts of town.

Imagine, if you can, what it must have been like to come from a warm fertile place where you and your family were known and respected, to a cold unknown land where you could not find your bearings.

A Letter Home

Write a letter home which you know you will not post, because you would not wish to worry your parents. Put in it all the things you would like to say, and then write a very different, much shorter letter containing what you would be willing to post home.

There'll Always Be a Welcome?

When you hear the older people's stories about their early years here, do you feel that Britain has improved its response to new immigrants? Can you find any newspaper reports of the arrival of Caribbean immigrants in the early 1950s – through your local library or on the internet – and compare them with what the tabloid newspapers are printing today about incomers?

Sorry, the Room Has Gone

Many story-tellers report on discrimination in housing. They were told rooms were available but, when they arrived, the accommodation was suddenly mysteriously full. Act out a scene in which this occurs. You could try to play it again with two people representing each character: one person saying what was actually said and the other saying what he or she felt, but could not say.

Nurses Needed

Look at the pictures of nurses in their uniform. Many of the immigrants who came here in the 1950s and 60s went into public services like health and transport. They had to wear the same uniforms as everyone else. Perhaps this helped others to see them as contributors in areas where they were needed. What skills are we short of in Britain today? How can we help new immigrants to integrate?

Come and Join Us

Design a poster campaign to attract workers to Britain to help in particular trades where there is a shortage of skilled workers, including plumbing and electrical work, teaching and medicine.

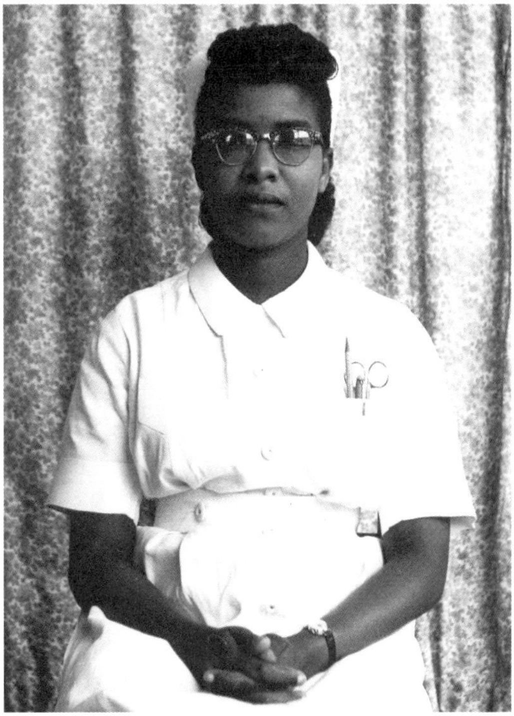

Dorothy Applethwaite, who came from Guyana to work as a nurse

Chapter Six: Growing Old in Britain

CHINESE ELDERS

Mr Ke Wing Pang

When we retired, we gave our house in Harlow to our older son who is 44. He is working in a Chinese restaurant. The younger son lives in Tonbridge. He is in office admin-type work. He didn't want to go into restaurant work because the hours are long and there is not much money. My younger son says that with the type of work he does he can go to his office at 10.00 or 11.00am and come home at 5.00. Two of my children have had traditional Chinese weddings, the youngest one is not married. My daughter lives in Kwon Long, Hong Kong. She has a British passport so she can come back at any time.

I moved to Tonbridge for a while to stay with my younger son and daughter-in-law, but we found problems in living

together with the younger generation, so we moved to a sheltered housing scheme in Tonbridge. It was nice there, but it was a white sheltered scheme and we had difficulties with the language there. Nobody could help us with interpreting. So we have moved now to Kenneth Lee House which is a Chinese sheltered housing scheme in Greenwich. Moving in here, life is much better because there is more support. When you need to see the doctor you can get help with communicating because we have a manager here, Helen Kon, who speaks Chinese.

My wife and I go back to Hong Kong every ten years. I wouldn't want to live there now, because I find it too hot and I have got used to the climate here. There are so many new buildings there and it has changed a lot. I don't always feel safe in Hong Kong either, because sometimes the security is not very good and there is a lot of thieving. It is not so rough here and it is also better for my health. When my asthma is coming I normally get the doctor to come here or I get the car and go to the hospital. But in Hong Kong that isn't possible, you have to wait for hours. And in Hong Kong when you have to go to the hospital you have to pay a lot of money. My wife is in Hong Kong at the moment. She has gone to look after her mother who is ill.

I do miss the open house approach to life in Hong Kong, where everyone comes and goes and there is always someone visiting. In this country you are all working at different times and having holidays at different times, so you don't see each other that often. My older brother is living here in London, in Leytonstone, so we do sometimes meet up in Chinatown. But I sometimes feel sad because I don't see my grandchildren that often. Their upbringing is very different to how I was raised. The youngest, nine years old, doesn't understand Cantonese, only English. But they like the food even though they don't know what it should taste like. My sons have an understanding of the culture but the grandchildren will gradually forget or not know because they have never been back. It is a pity, but there is nothing we can do about it; it is up to them. We can't force them and it is more important for their future that they know English so well.

Mrs Phuong La

When my husband passed away, I moved to Kenneth Lee Sheltered Housing for Chinese-Vietnamese people. I have never returned to Vietnam, but I do sometimes go back to China and Hong Kong to visit for a holiday. I have no relatives left over there since my sister passed away, and the house I used to live in has been torn down and has been replaced with a 20-storey building. There is still lots of thieving in Macao. I visited in 2001 and it was very bad.

I feel more at home in Britain now. The old and the young are better off here. In 1996 I went to America to see some friends. They were people who had been friends of my husband, from when they were teaching together back in China. Seeing how my friends lived in America made me realise how my situation here was better. My friends have no income support, and it is very difficult to get free medicine in America.

I live with other Chinese-Vietnamese elders. We play mah-jong, we have visits arranged for us to the market where I buy all my groceries and vegetables. I visit the Glyndon Community Centre which organises a luncheon club once a week. My son lives in Deptford and works in Peckham. He comes here to visit me and

Keeping up with traditions – Mrs Luong's altar, which she "prays to every day"

we speak on the phone a lot. When I was living in Newcastle I used to attend the Chinese Catholic church and I am still a practising Catholic. I am happy in my old age. I feel settled.

Mrs Ah Poh Luong

My husband and I stayed with my son and daughter-in-law at first, and then we moved to Hackney with my daughter and her husband. My husband and I were retired and spent our time meeting with friends and shopping. My son-in-law moved to Woolwich and I applied to the Council unsuccessfully for a house near them. When my husband died, I applied again because I so wanted to be near to my son. I tried for three years, and in the end, Greenwich Council Housing Department suggested that I come here to this Chinese Vietnamese sheltered housing unit. So I have been here for some years. I am used to it and I know how to find my way around.

I try and keep myself busy. I don't see my family as often as I would like, and sometimes I get lonely and bored. The grandchildren are all grown up. I go and see them sometimes. It is funny when I think how different my life has been from theirs. They don't really know about my life on the boat as a girl, or what I went through later on. They don't know about Chinese history, but my children do. I keep up with some of my traditions. I have an altar in my living room which I pray to every day. One day, I hope to get a nice cupboard so I can really arrange it properly. I play mah-jong with other people living here. I go to the market to buy Chinese vegetables.

I do sometimes go back to China to visit my brother and his family who are still there. I sometimes visit friends and relations in America as well. But, on reflection, I feel here is my home, especially after the Vietnam war. It is right to put my roots down here. I am now so old. I don't know how many years I have left. It is nice to have shared my story with someone.

Mrs Suk Tsang Tang

My husband, one of my daughters and my younger son stayed on in Vietnam. My oldest son applied for a family reunion for the whole family to get here, but the problem was that the youngest son wasn't allowed to come because he was already married in Vietnam. And when you're married, you're considered to be independent so you can't go with the parents. So the younger son is still in Vietnam now. But the two daughters are here and in the end, my husband also managed to come here to England, but he died last year. It took a long time to get the whole family here for a family reunion.

I live in a nice new house in Surrey Quays in Bermondsey. When we arrived we all lived together, me, my daughters and my grandchildren. But they've got married now. They live elsewhere. One is in Camden Town, and one is near me in Bermondsey.

My children and grandchildren have a good chance to make a success of life in England. My son is a dim sum chef that we mentioned earlier. One of my daughters is an interpreter in a doctor's surgery. One is a housewife.

My grandchildren speak Chinese. They go to school in Bermondsey. I am very happy with the situation. I have felt very welcome. English people are very nice. I've made good friends here and I enjoy coming to this centre. I still do sewing in the house working from home for English people. They have a factory. People bring the work to me, and come to collect it when it's finished; trousers, skirts, jackets.

AFRICAN ELDERS

Mrs Belmont Williams

I lived in the United States of America for about eight years after I retired from the Sierra Leone Civil Service. However, because of my age, I felt it was time I lived at least in the same part of the world with my daughter. I therefore relocated to Britain at the end of 1997. I am spending my time doing voluntary work in the community. When I lived with my daughter in the Borough of Waltham Forest I served with Age Concern visiting one afternoon a week an 85 years old English woman who lived alone. I was also a member of the Management Committee of the League of Friends of Whipps Cross Hospital. I was involved with fund raising to provide much-needed equipment for the hospital. I also volunteered for an organisation providing services to refugees.

I moved to Woolwich in the Borough of Greenwich in 1999 and I have been involved in several voluntary activities there. I am the co-founder and was the first chair of the Greenwich Ajoda Organisation for older African people. I have been blessed with friends and relations, so I have been able to socialise quite a lot, including various celebrations such as birthdays, traditional activities and weddings. I am a Christian, so I attend Church services fairly regularly and participate in the various festivities and programmes in the Church's calendar.

I am comfortable in my present house. Unfortunately my beautiful home in Freetown was destroyed by fire started by the rebels in January 1999. Consequently I am homeless in my own country. When I went home in 2001 to attend the funeral of my only brother, I had to stay with my cousin.

Mrs Josephine Macpeppele Ja Ja

I have been living in London for three years now. I am still ill and I have trouble walking but I take tablets for it. All my grandchildren are here. I've got a great-grandchild too. A girl, I've seen her, a pretty girl, her name is Montana.

I have got used to the weather here too. Where I live, everyone is helpful, and the people are kind, but they don't go to church. If you start talking about church, they'll leave you. They say they don't believe in it. But without Christ, I don't know where I would be now. Religion is very important to me. But in Nigeria I'm a member of the Pentecostal Church. As a child of God, I feel I'm everything, British, Nigerian, we're all one.

I would like to go back to Nigeria for a holiday, but I can't live there, I can't afford it. So for now, this is my home. When I die, they'll take me to Nigeria and bury me in the cemetery at Port Harcourt. The old tradition is to bury people in their houses back home, but my children don't like that idea, so I will be buried in a cemetery.

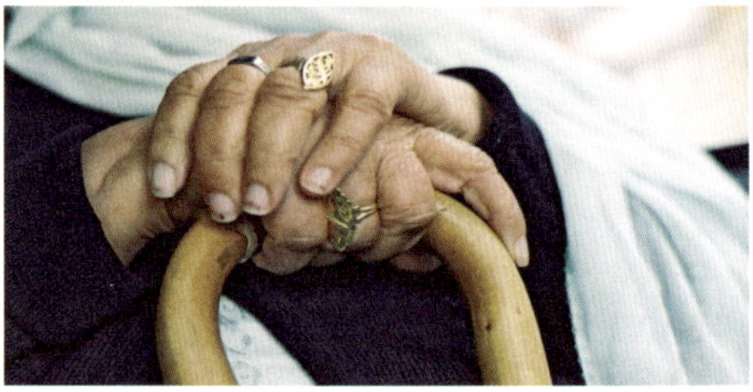

Mr James Adebayo Adesina
I returned here in 1994, but I will tell you I cannot live in this country. So I have been here just under ten years, my second coming! I'm retired now and I do voluntary jobs for the council. I'm on some panels like Greenwich Borough Council. I think it is important to give something back to society, because society has given us something. Although I keep myself busy I don't feel settled because we Africans, we are gregarious. I don't want to be in this place and die in this place without people beside me. I think probably as an African, I would be better off spending my old age in my native land than remaining here. What future does an elderly person have when you are frightened in your own home? I'm not saying that Nigeria is completely safe but if we can go back home and spend our old age where we belong, so much the better. When I see some elderly people here, people who live in this block, they are lucky and I'm happy for that, but many of these elderly people are also going into homes. I go home for three or four months. I want to go to celebrate my

seventieth birthday next year. I hope to have a party with all my friends and family.

I don't have to worry about my children because they are settled down, I consider myself open-mined in relation to my children's choices. One of my sons is married to an Italian, another son is married to a Ghanaian. My first son married a girl from the Eastern part of Nigeria. I consider myself the United Nations! I have nothing against mixed marriages as long as the couple are in love, and as long as they know what they are doing. Who am I to put divisions? Good luck to them – it is their own life!

There are some very good things that one needs to learn from this country, but to me, the future is what I am a little bit worried about. Because sometimes I have a little bit of trouble with the boys in my neighbourhood who disturb the elderly; people as old as eighty-five or going on ninety. We all take care of each other. Back home it is like a compound, all the elderly stick together. I am lucky because I have the opportunity of going back to Nigeria, I don't want to end up in a residential home here, so I think I will go home when I am very old. The government have not realised in time that this is a multicultural society now. All the people living in this country must all work together to make it a better place. There must be tolerance for the multicultural groups in order that everyone can enjoy living in harmony.

Mrs Mako Herabe

I now live in New Cross in south east London. I don't do a great deal; just sitting and waiting to see what life will bring. I still have links back home. Every two or three days I have people calling from Somalia who were left behind, asking for help. So I am I here and there in a way, because I think so much about home and members of my family who are still over there. I am considered the caretaker of the house because my daughter works. So I take care of the grandchildren and speak on the phone, and I do look forward to visitors. Mostly we only meet up on big occasions when, God forbid, someone dies, or if there is a marriage, or someone has a child. Those are the only opportunities for me to mix.

I still uphold my traditions. We eat traditional food and I am still dressing the same. I go with my daughter when she is shopping in Deptford. That is the only time I go out.

I do miss my home I would like to go back home one day. I am praying not to die here because I am very scared about being buried in a coffin. Back home we do not bury people in coffins; we wrap the person in special clothes and put them straight in the ground. What they say in Somalia is, "it is very hot so why put them in a box?" So I pray that one day I will go back home.

Mrs Irma Reid

I stopped nursing when I became sick. I suffered with a bad back, high blood pressure, maybe from carrying those suitcases when I first came over! I am sure that I have got strained shoulders from lifting heavy patients over all the years of nursing.

I have lived in Woolwich since 1984. My mum has come over three times since I have been living here. The last time she came was in 1995. She was eighty-one years old then and she was a bit absent minded. My dad had not long died and I think she was disorientated. We took her out on a few visits, but we didn't have a car so that was a bit difficult. She was here for six months and then when she went back home, she was back to her normal self. Old people often tend to get disoriented when they go to a strange place, especially to a strange country, and I think she felt better at home in Trinidad. My dad never came. He never left Trinidad after he went there from Tobago when he was twenty-one, and the only two times he returned to Tobago was for his mother's funeral and his father's funeral and that was it. All my brothers and sisters have been to visit me here.

I live with my sister and my daughter Victoria who is 23. My other sister lives in New Jersey, and the rest are back in Jamaica. I don't dislike living here. I like living in England. I think basically we have never had any problems over here. I would like to go back maybe once a year or every two years or so and come back for six months of the year.

Irma Reid enjoying Christmas 2003 at her London home

Mr Michael Roper

I live with my wife in London. All my children are grown up and settled here as well. I have two girls and one boy. I am very close to my children and my daughters are always round to visit us. It is funny, but I am sure one of my daughter's twin sons has taken after me. He is a bit of a genius and he is only four! Both twins are really bright. I remember one time we were at the barbers and one of the twins was looking at the pictures of different countries and calling out their names. Everyone was amazed.

Now that I am retired, I live off my pension. All those years I worked so hard have finally paid off. About three times a week I spend the day at Elford Close, which is an African Caribbean Day Centre. It is a lively place where Caribbean and African elders mix together. We talk, have a laugh, watch television and every lunchtime we get fed lovely Caribbean food.

Mrs Gladys Smith

I like living in London. I like the freedom about it, because you can please yourself, live to your full capacity without over-stepping it. I live within my means and I'm happy here, very happy here. And you know, people have the idea that you must expand, people want to get richer and have a bigger house. I don't envy anyone. The Council gave me this flat and when I saw it I was so happy, so glad because it was in the spring and this place was lovely – very, very nice. The lawn was beautiful, the garden was lovely. When the girl from the Council came to show me the flat, she didn't know that my mind was already made up! So she's telling me, "I do hope you will like it." I tried not to be over-zealous, you know. I said, "Yes, it will be fine, we could try with it." So I am still here now, 13 years later, thank God.

Traditional Caribbean kitchenware

Mrs Avtar Bilkhu

I live in Plumstead with my daughter and my mother-in-law. One of my sons lives across the street from me and one lives in Clapton. One is in Hounslow with his wife and two kids. My daughter took after me. She is ambitious and did a law degree. I wanted her to learn, that's what life is about. My husband passed away six years ago. He had an accident in the car. He was a nice, good man. He worked really hard when he was alive. He tried many business ventures: three shops, a takeaway, a butcher's shop and a grocery shop, but all of them went down the drain.

I took after my uncle and I have kept up my community interests. I am very active in the Sikh community, as president of the women's committee at the Ramgharia Sikh Temple, and I also teach young children the mother tongue, which I have been doing for 20 years now. I take my religion and culture seriously. It is part of me, but I don't impose it on others. They have to do it by themselves. I read books, I play the harmonium and sing. I normally play at the Gurdwara and sometimes I play at home by myself.

I consider this country to be my home. If my children and grandchildren were not here, it would be different. I get on well with everyone and I am friendly to everybody. I still go back to India for holidays and to see my relatives. I am now thinking of selling the home I still have in India, because I am living here which is a better place for elderly people. Health is everything, and here you have free facilities and access to doctors. You have to pay for medicine over there and life can be difficult for that reason.

There are three generations of my family living in Britain now, so I am happy. I am the head of the family, my husband gave me that responsibility. He never interfered, he trusted me.

Mrs Bilkhu playing the harmonium at the Ramgharia Sikh temple, Woolwich

Mr Fazal Rahim Shah

I kept the handbag-making business going for forty years and then I handed it over to my sons. I've never been unemployed. I never claimed anything until I retired. I consider Britain my home. I arrived in 1960, and I changed my nationality in 1963 from Pakistani to British. The reason was that I used to go to different fashion shows on the continent where our handbags were being shown. And being a Pakistani passport holder, it was very difficult for me every time I had to apply for a visa. Some countries would grant you one and others wouldn't. So I argued with the Home Office and told them the problem. And they said, under these special circumstances, they would grant me a British passport and dual nationality.

My eldest son is in the handbag business near Southend, and he has got his own house. The second son is a manager in Safeway stores. And the third one is doing his A-levels. I take them home to Pakistan every year. I have a home there, with the same facilities as here, a similar house. And I have a car there. Now I spend five months, six, seven months a year in Pakistan. I spend the winter there and the summer here. My wife's family left her some land. They are a very well-known family in Pakistan, as army officers and landowners. I am very close to my in-laws over there. We phone every week, to talk to our families. We don't write now like we used to; we phone. And I have land there too. I lease my land to someone, because I can't look after it myself. I go back to the village when I can and collect whatever I have to.

Mr Shah visiting family in Pakistan

All my siblings have built houses along one street. The whole piece of land belonged to my father, and he divided it into four parts. And I built on mine, and my other brothers built on theirs. The other two brothers live in theirs. My children are not interested in going to Pakistan to live at the moment. But whenever they go, they have a house there, they have a servant, they have a car there. They can go and live there any time.

Now I'm very busy with community work. I have many meetings: I am a police adviser, I go to council meetings, and Community Health meetings. I'm an executive member of the Greenwich Council for Racial Equality. I also run an Asian Community Hall – I'm the secretary there. So I'm involved in loads of activities. I got involved in community work because I was interested in Asian welfare, especially older Asian people. We are trying to get a home for older Asians, to acquire it from the council and then go on from there.

In this country, Asian women – especially older Indian and Pakistani women – are the most neglected group and nobody cares two bits about it. The government doesn't provide, social services don't provide. Women are getting sick by sitting at home, they are getting fat, having diabetes heart problems. Asian men and women have 60% of the diabetes in this country. And the basic reason is that they don't have activities; they don't have anywhere to go. I'm talking about the first generation. Because they were economic migrants, they spent their whole strength earning money. Everyone got money and wealth, they bought houses, but they lacked social outlets, cultural opportunities and English language skills, so their isolation now is a problem we are trying to address.

The daughters of these first generation women have got married and gone away. The boys don't want to live with their parents, even though there might have room enough. They want privacy, they want to live on their own, so they spread out. I don't blame them, but what happens is that the old people get left out. Like me in this house, there's just me and my wife and my son. So the extended family is disappearing, which is a shame. And our aim is to provide for the old, especially the women.

I don't regret a single minute of coming here. I'm very happy. I'm very comfortable and very happy. My sons are educated and doing very well. I have no problems. I consider that I have the best of both countries and both feel like home to me. I hold a dual nationality and that's how I feel. I am British through and through, and I am Pakistani also.

Mrs Pramila Desai

I have my own house with my husband, and my son often comes to visit us. I spend a lot of my time in community centres and so does my husband. He is retired and he likes to visit friends and he does the shopping for me.

A few years ago, I helped to open an Asian centre in the old Play Tower building in Lewisham to help older people, Muslims and Hindus, who were sad and lonely. We only opened one day each week, and then that centre closed down because the whole building was condemned as unsafe. We cried and protested and everything, but there was nothing we could do.

Then I worked with the older people doing social work. I never studied or

Pramila outside her home in London

anything, but I just learned through practical experience. I am still working as a carer you know. I care for one elderly person now; she is an Indian lady and I go to get her medicine and heat up her food as she cannot do things on her own and she is living all alone in a big house.

I first went back to India after 32 years in this country. It was completely different from how I remembered it; so modern now. But I prefer living in this country, partly because of my diabetes; the treatment would not be so good over there. I think I may go over again next year, but just to visit, you know.

I have good friends nearby and we all help each other. And I have friends at the Saheli Women's Group which meets every week in Woolwich. There are now so many traditional celebrations and cultural events, so many temples and Gurdwara that I almost feel I am living in India. We have everything here now. I do feel at home here.

Mrs Sheila Rakhit

At present, I have completed my teaching career and I am enjoying my retirement, except for some small physical ailments which give me cause for concern. I know life today is full of stress and tension and that stress can damage our life, our minds and bodies, so we must be warned and change our lifestyle. I have done this. I think it is necessary to learn to relax, to take time out, to unlock tension. My weekly regime now is going to keep fit and aqua-aerobics classes and I have got involved with many voluntary organisations and this way I give back something and I find that very rewarding.

My entire journey of life – as a little girl, a student, a young woman, a wife, a mother, and a teacher and as an older woman – was not a bed of roses. I had to cross many obstacles. At some places I stumbled, but at some I sailed through. To tell you the truth, I think I have done fairly well, considering that I had to come from the other side of the world. Coming to the end of my travels across the world, and thinking about the course my life has taken, I'll be honest with you and say I look back with mixed feelings. It does come in one's mind sometimes how things might have been. But I made this country my home, I have lived here for thirty-six years, and I am happy, you know, as I am. Now I feel that I should contribute my share of real-life experiences and knowledge, for the benefit of anyone who will read about it in the future. I believe that I have some words of wisdom, and I hope that my story might be useful, interesting and helpful for some, who might find it in sharp contrast to the present day and their own experience.

Growing Old in Britain Creative Activities

OLDER PEOPLE'S ACTIVITIES

Health Matters

Many of the story-tellers speak of their health in this chapter. Having access to free medicine is vitally important for them. How do they rate the service they receive from their local GP, clinic or hospital?

Highs and Lows

Looking back over their lives, can the older people pick out the really significant 'high points' (and maybe a few low points too) by marking them above and below a life line representing the different decades? This can be expanded to include photos, certificates and maps to make a personal life display board.

Life Portraits

A variant on this activity is to help the older people to make a Life Portrait Box. This can be in a special wooden box, or even just a supermarket box, and it can show the memories which matter to the teller through photos and captions, small mementos, press cuttings, etc. Really ambitious box designers can add light and sound to the box using hidden CDs and wiring the box to a plug.

Desert Island Discs

What are the songs of home which have stayed with people through their lives? Arrange a 'Desert Island Discs' session for each member of the group and sing through or play recorded versions of best-loved music and its associations. Sometimes a group can co-operate to find all the words of a well-loved song, where the individual can only remember a line or two. This is a pleasurable activity for small groups and opens up opportunities for singing together and sharing memories.

Ages Apart

Some of the story-tellers express great concern about the language and culture gap which has opened up between themselves and the younger generations in their families. What do group members feel about their children's language ability? And their grandchildren's?

Take Me Home
Burial customs are clearly very different from one culture to another. It is important to some of our story-tellers to be taken to their home country for burial and for all the correct rituals to be observed. What do group members feel about this matter? What do they think are the implications for their families of their wishes with regard to their funerals? Have they written out their wishes? What would they be if they did?

A Place of Our Own
How important do members of the group feel it is to provide separate facilities for ethnic minority elders? What do they see as the pros and cons of separate provision? Write these out in two columns on a large piece of paper and compare opinions?

Meals & Menus
What is their experience of using general services such as social services day centres and meals on wheels? If they could give advice to the meals-on-wheels providers about what they prepare, what would they ask for? Prepare some menus which would please the group. Maybe even send them to the local providers.

Whose Responsibility?
How far do the elders in the group feel that their care should be the responsibility of their families and communities, and how far should the state provide? Do they think their children would give the same answers to these questions?

Pride
Do members of the group enjoy wearing traditional clothes associated with their home background? When do they feel it is important to be dressed in a traditional way and when do they feel it is not important or appropriate?

When I Am Old

Health is a very important issue to the elders speaking in this chapter. Older people are prime users of the health services, and have free access to medicine and treatment. Discuss in the class whether you think there will still be a National Health Service there for you when you are old?

Together or Separate?

Special community groups and services, often supported by social services departments, are being established for ethnic minority elders. What do you think of this development? Discuss the pros and cons of separate provision in your group.

The Story of My Life

The story-tellers in the book have talked about different stages of their lives in chronological sequence. School students have not lived through so much but there is still plenty to remember. Write down some of your earliest memories, people you have been close to, special events and exciting journeys. This could be in the form of a lifeline with dates along it. Or you could choose to try writing a poem which tells in short phrases the moments you wish to recall and remember.

You may discover that it is quite painful to think about some of the sad things that have happened in your life so far, and you may want to pass over them quickly. Talk to another person about how that feels, and then consider together some of the sad stories told by the elders in this book. They will have had to revisit some painful memories too during their interviews, but they still wished to participate because they wanted a record of their lives to survive.

A Life Story Interview & Book

If a grandparent or another older person is willing to come to the classroom to talk about his or her life, you could conduct a life story interview. Follow the chapter headings in the book and prepare some questions to ask. Be sure these are open questions, and not the sort which require a yes or no answer or a single word answer. You may like to divide into groups and let each group take responsibility for asking about one section of the older person's life. Write down what you remember and illustrate it with your idea of what the people and places in the story looked like. Then invite the older person back to enjoy the end result.

What I Miss Most

What do you think it would be like to grow old far from where you grew up? If you were to spend your later years in a faraway country, what do think would be your strongest memories of Britain and what would you miss the most? How might you hold on to some of your own culture, even if you knew you could never come back?

Background Reading on Reminiscence

PRACTICAL GUIDES

Lifetimes: Photocards, Memories, Ideas for Reminiscence
by Pam Schweitzer (1987) Age Exchange

The Reminiscence Handbook: Ideas for Creative Activities with Older People
by Caroline Osborn (1993) Age Exchange

Age Exchanges: Reminiscence Projects for Children and Older People
by Pam Schweitzer (1993) Age Exchange

Reminiscence – Social and Creative Activities with Older People
by Roger Sim (1997) Winslow Press

Reminiscence and Recall: A Guide to Good Practice
by Faith Gibson (1998) Age Concern Books

Reminiscing with People with Dementia: A Handbook for Carers
by Errollyn Bruce, Sarah Hodgson, & Pam Schweitzer (1999) Age Exchange

The Reminiscence Trainer's Pack
by Faith Gibson (2000) Age Concern Books

Talking in Class
by Alan Redfern (1996) Oral History Society

A Time To Share: Powerful Personal Stories for Teaching History & Citizenship
by David Savill (2002) Age Exchange

WRITINGS ABOUT REMINISCENCE

Reminiscence in Dementia Care
ed. Pam Schweitzer (1998) Age Exchange

The Past in the Present: Reminiscence in Health and Social Care by Faith Gibson (2004) Health Professions Press, Baltimore

The Therapeutic Purposes of Reminiscence
by Mike Bender, Paulette Baukham and Andrew Norris (1999) Sage Publications

The Art and Science of Reminiscing
by Barbara Haight and Jeffrey Webster (1995) Taylor & Francis, USA

Age, Race and Ethnicity
ed. Ken Blakemore and Margaret Boneham (1994) Open University Press

Reminiscence Reviewed ed. Joanna Bornat (1994) Open University Press

Ageing and Reminiscence Processes
by Peter Coleman (1986) John Wiley

Useful Contacts

Age Exchange Reminiscence Centre
(See page 2)

The Oral History Society
c/o Department of History
Essex University, Colchester CO4 3SQ
tel 020 7412 7405, email rob.perks@bl.uk
www.oralhistory.org.uk

Commission for Racial Equality
St Dunstan's House
201 – 211 Borough High Street
London SE1 1GZ, tel 020 7939 0000
fax 020 7939 0001, email info@cre.gov.uk
www.cre.gov.uk

Black Cultural Archives
378 Coldharbour Lane, London SW9 8RR
tel 020 7738 4591, fax 020 7738 7168
email info@aambh.co.uk

Mckenzie Heritage Pictures
Studio 226, Station House
49 Greenwich High Road
London SE10 8JL, tel 020 8469 2000
email info@mckenziehpa.com
www.mckenziehpa.com

The UK Reminiscence Network
c/o Age Exchange Reminiscence Centre
(See page 2)
www.reminiscence-network.org.uk

Useful Websites

Age Exchange
www.age-exchange.org.uk

Moving Here:
200 Years of Migration to England
www.movinghere.org.uk

British Library National Sound Archive
Oral History/National Life Story Collection
www.bl.uk

BBC Education
History – 20th Century Vox
www.bbc.co.uk/education/20cvox/

Department of Sound Records
Imperial War Museum, London
www.iwm.org.uk/lambeth/sound.htm

Ethnic Communities Oral History Project
www.hfusc.org.uk/ecohp

Mass Observation Archive
University of Sussex
www.sussex.ac.uk/library/massobs/homearch.html

Refugee Action
www.refugee-action.org

Age Exchange Publications

Our books provide a highly entertaining and educational way of exploring living memory. They are lively and easy to read, conversational in style and lavishly illustrated with photographs and line drawings of the time. The stories are told in the original words of the older people we have interviewed over the last 20 years, edited to help the reader to a clear sense of the period under discussion and the personality of the speaker.

A Place To Stay
A unique collection of reflections by elders from many ethnic groups who have settled in Britain. Their frank and often poignant stories are told in English and in the speakers' original languages: Chinese, Hindi, Gujerati, Punjabi, Greek, Turkish, Polish and Italian. 64 pages (A4) £4.

Across The Irish Sea
London Irish older people remember their childhood in Ireland and their decision to 'cross the water'. They describe their experience of finding work and homes over here, reflecting on their continuing relationship with Ireland. 175 pages (A5) £5.

All Our Christmases
The perfect Christmas present for older readers. Pensioners recall late-night Christmas shopping, making their own decorations, the ritual of Christmas pudding stirring and wishing, the last minute search for a turkey at a knockdown price, the Christmas meal and the festivities which followed. A complete guide to Christmas past. 24 pages (A4) £2.

Can We Afford The Doctor?
This book examines health and social welfare in the early part of this century when people often had to rely on their own resources and remedies to cope with illness or disability. 80 pages (A4) £4.

A Day At The Fair
A collection of hilarious memories of going to the fair on Bank Holidays in the 1920s and 30s. 32 pages (A5)£1.

Fifty Years Ago
Life in the early 1930s through the recollections of elderly people in South East London including unemployment, first jobs, marches and demonstrations, the cinema, courting days, and illness and holidays. 48 pages (A4) £3.

Footprints In The Sand
Seaside memories of the 1930s and 40s with delightful holiday snaps of the time. 64 pages (A5) £3.

Good Morning Children
Schooldays in the 1920s and 30s. Fascinating reading and delightful photographs for today's and yesterday's school children. 56 pages (A4) £4.

Goodnight Children Everywhere
A remarkable collection of first hand experiences of evacuation in the Second World War. The contributors speak honestly, in many cases for the first time, about the upheaval they went through as children, illustrating their stories with letters they wrote at the time and the photos of themselves which were taken to send home to their parents. With over 250 superb photographs. 256 pages (A4 landscape) £15.

Grandmother's Footsteps
Older people remember their grandparents who were born during the reign of Queen Victoria and who were known by the writers during their childhoods in the 1920s and 30s. 66 pages (A5) £3.

Health Remedies and Healthy Recipes
Reflections by Caribbean elders on the subject of health and diet as remembered in the West Indies and experienced here in Britain. 24 pages (A4) £4.

Jubilee
Memories and photos of the early 1950s, a play text based on these and other memories, and a detailed description of the improvisation and rehearsal process involved in creating a play with a group of older people from their own reminiscences. 88 pages (A5) £3.

Living Through The Blitz
Londoners' memories of broken nights in and out of the shelter, being bombed out, hazardous journeys to work, queuing for rationed food and hunting for shrapnel among the ruins. 56 pages (A5) £4.

My First Job
An anthology of memories and photographs from older people who started work between 1912 and 1940. 32 pages (A4) £3.

On The River
The recollections of older Londoners who have lived by and worked on the River Thames. Their stories recapture the sense of bustle and industry when the river was London's main thoroughfare and a crucial source of livelihood for thousands of families. The book contains over 100 full page photographs of the river in its heyday. 184 pages (A4 landscape) £15.

Our Lovely Hops
Memories of hop-picking in Kent, plus over 100 delightful photos of work and play 'down hopping'. 112 pages (A4) £7.

The Time of Our Lives
A compilation of memories and photos of leisure time and courting days in the 1920s and 1930s. 64 pages (A4) £4.

What Did You Do In The War, Mum?
The story of women's work and lives during the First and especially the Second World Wars. At this time, a whole new range of activities suddenly became open to women. This book tells how they coped. 72 pages (A4) £5.

When the Lights Go On Again

Older people from south London remember VE Day and rebuilding family life at the end of World War II. 52 pages (A5) £3.

REMINISCENCE HANDBOOKS AND ACTIVITY PACKS

Age Exchanges

A handbook of reminiscence projects for children and older people to try together. Suggestions are offered as to how the activities described relate to the National Curriculum. All the ideas can be adapted for use in classrooms or community settings. 65 pages (A4) £7.50.

A Time To Share

Powerful personal stories for teaching history and citizenship. Each story is followed by suggested classroom activities to help school children understand their own rights and responsibilities through learning about older people's experience of the past. 64 pages(A4) £9.95.

Lifetimes

This reminiscence pack provides first class support material for people wishing to develop recall work with groups of older people. It includes a 68-page handbook full of activities and ideas for discussion around reminiscence themes, plus many 'starter memories' to get discussion going. There are 4 copies of each double-sided laminated and enlarged photo, so that different members of the group can all be looking at the same photo.
68 pages plus 60 Picture Cards (A4) £30.

The Reminiscence Handbook

"A splendidly practical 'how to do it' book which contains innumerable suggestions about how to encourage older people to recall their own past and to share their rich recollections with others." – Professor Faith Gibson, University of Ulster. This manual is a must for those starting a reminiscence programme and anyone looking for tried and tested ideas around key reminiscence themes.
104 pages (A4) £9.95.

Reminiscing with People with Dementia
"This manual will give a new impetus to carers who are looking for positive ways to engage with those they care for." Dr Nori Graham, Chair, Alzheimers Disease International. This new handbook for carers contains a wealth of practical ideas and suggestions for using reminiscence to enrich communication with people with dementia. It is illustrated with delightful photographs from the many European partners of Age Exchange who participated in this international dementia project. 104 pages (A4) £9.95.

Reminiscence in Dementia Care
Articles by international experts who came together at a conference in London organised by Age Exchange, promoting imaginative and humane approaches to dementia care using reminiscence and life review. 158 pages (A5) £9.95.

To order any of the above titles or packs, please contact Age Exchange *(see page 2)**.*